How to Grow
BULBS

*By the Editors of Sunset Books
and Sunset Magazine*

LANE BOOKS · MENLO PARK, CALIFORNIA

ACKNOWLEDGMENTS

In revising this book, we utilized the knowledge of commercial bulb growers as well as home gardeners who especially enjoy growing bulbs. We extend our thanks to the following individuals: Pat Antonelli, begonia grower, Santa Cruz, California; John E. Bryan, Director, Strybing Arboretum, San Francisco, California; Gladys Coffee, begonia grower, Capitola, California; Jerry Davids, bulb grower, Los Angeles, California; Joe Davis, bulb grower, Puyallup, Washington; Dr. August De Hertogh, Professor of Horticulture, Michigan State University, East Lansing, Michigan; Fred Delkin, bulb grower, Bellevue, Washington; Alice Gans, bulb grower, Arcadia, California; E. J. Hamilton, dahlia grower; Santa Clara, California; Edgar Kline, bulb grower, Lake Grove, Oregon; Gerry Mahieu, Netherlands National Tourist Office, San Francisco, California; Dr. Henry P. Orr, Professor of Ornamental Horticulture, Auburn University, Auburn, Alabama; Fred H. Petersen, Soil and Plant Laboratory, Santa Clara, California; Mrs. Rolfe W. Smith, Longwood Gardens, Kennett Square, Pennsylvania; Ray Whitcomb, lily grower, Gresham, Oregon.

Edited by Gail Knight Wentzell

Special Consultant: John R. Dunmire, Assistant Editor, *Sunset* Magazine

Design: John Flack

Illustrations: E. D. Bills

Cover: Darwin Hybrid Tulips. Photography by Ells Marugg.

Executive Editor, Sunset Books: David E. Clark

Contents

Introduction to bulbs **4**

        a long and glamorous history

What is a bulb? **6**

        drawings and descriptions of bulbs, corms, rhizomes, tuberous roots, and tubers

Growing healthy bulbs **8**

        growth requirements; growing bulbs in containers; diseases and pests

Ways to use bulbs **13**

        in landscaping; in pots to bring indoors; in flower arrangements; in combination with other plants; in containers on patios

Miniatures **20**

        the little children of the bulb world

AN ENCYCLOPEDIA OF BULBS **23**

        from Achimenes to Zephyranthes

Special Features

    Holland: largest bulb garden in the world 5
    Plants listed according to type of bulb 7
    Forcing: anticipate spring with bulbs 11
    Naturalizing: follow nature's example 18

Introduction to Bulbs

. . . a long and glamorous history

Bulbs are beloved for their beauty, whether you prefer the delicate scilla, the flamboyant canna, the fragrant hyacinth, the stately lily, or the colorful tulip. The better we become acquainted with bulbs, the more we marvel at the variety of their colors and forms. And the longer we grow bulbs, the more we appreciate the certainty and ease with which you can use them to create satisfying garden color schemes.

The bulbs of spring are especially dear: these first bulbs flower when the world is eager for color. You can plant bulbs to continue this display through the hottest part of the year and on into autumn; some bulbs will even blossom during winter in mild climates or on an indoor windowsill.

Bulbs have a long and glamorous history as garden plants. Frescoes and vases decorated with lily motifs have been discovered in the relics of ancient Crete, dating from 1800 or 1600 B.C. Records show that the Pharaohs grew anemones in their gardens and that narcissus and lilies were used by the ancient Egyptians in their funeral wreaths. Solomon, of the Old Testament, had a garden containing lilies and crocus. As early as 380 B.C., the Greeks were using crocus, lilies, and hyacinths in ceremonial crowns, and the philosopher and botanist Theophrastus, in about 340 B.C., writes of alliums, anemones, crocus, cyclamen, gladiolus, grape hyacinths, lilies, narcissus, ranunculus, and scillas. Together with hyacinths and narcissus, lilies had an important place in the gardens of the early Romans, who valued these flowers for their use in religious ceremonies. The poet Virgil (70-19 B.C.) wrote several poems mentioning the lily, and it was he who made it a symbol of virginity. Then in the Middle Ages the lily was so cherished that it became a symbol of purity in the Church.

A CARICATURE of the Chariot of Flora during the "tulipomania" that raged in Holland from 1634 to 1637.

DETAIL of a 17th century painting by Jacob van Hulsdonck includes Rembrandt tulips, daffodils, fritillary.

The iris has a regal background. It is the fleur-de-lis that was the symbol of the kings of France for centuries. We love the dainty crocus in our gardens, but it is hardly as significant in our commerce as was the saffron crocus (*C. sativas*) to the Minoans of Crete, who sold the scented stigmas as a drug at fancy prices throughout the world.

Tulips were introduced to Western Europe during the Renaissance by Ogier de Busbecq, ambassador from the Holy Roman Emperor Ferdinand I to the court of Sultan Suleiman I. After seeing tulips in a garden near Constantinople, where they had been brought from Persia, Busbecq obtained seeds and took them to Vienna in 1554.

It wasn't until 1601, when the Flemish botanist Clusius introduced some tulip bulbs to the Netherlands, that bulbs became widely popular in Europe. Owning an unusual bulb became a status symbol; royalty and rich merchants paid tremendously large sums of money for a single bulb. In 1634 the craze mounted so high that it created a speculative orgy called "tulipomania" in Holland. Bulbs with blotched or feathered blooms brought fabulous prices: one variety of which there were only two bulbs sold for 5,500 florins (about $3,080). When the inevitable crash came in 1637, many were bankrupted. Although the price of bulbs fell, the demand for bulb flowers grew and continues today.

The modern, large-flowered gladiolus had its beginnings in 1841 when the Van Houttes introduced *Gladiolus gandavensis*. Hyacinths enjoyed popularity in Holland during the 18th century, when a bulb with an especially beautiful bloom brought the equivalent of $20,300. Then in the 19th century in France, a prized dahlia was traded for a rare diamond.

CROCUS in a fanciful Mexican clay pot were brought indoors during bloom to adorn the breakfast table.

HOLLAND: LARGEST BULB GARDEN IN THE WORLD

In the Netherlands, bulbs have grown from a 16th century novelty into a 20th century economic staple. Today, Dutch growers offer 800 varieties of tulips, as well as about 40 other kinds of bulbs, including hyacinth, narcissus, crocus, and gladiolus. And within each kind the varieties are numerous: 500 varieties of narcissus, 30 different hyacinths, and 30 varieties of the crocus. Bulb production accounts for over $100 million in the Dutch economy.

Holland grows bulbs on only 25,000 acres in the narrow North Sea sand dunes between Haarlem and Leyden. The famed Keukenhof is the center of this activity in the early spring, with approximately 10 million flowering bulbs on exhibit in outdoor plantings and in greenhouses. Keukenhof was never intended as a tourist attraction; it's a 60-acre showcase for the products of the 80 growers who participate in the operation.

Dutch bulb growers sell cut flowers of bulbous plants at Aalsmeer, the world's largest and most modern flower auction. The flowers arrive by barge; the buyers bid for flower lots; then the flowers are packed for immediate shipment.

LAVISH DISPLAYS of tulips and daffodils line the banks of a stream at Keukenhof Gardens in Holland.

What is a bulb?

. . . a bulb is a bulb, but not always

If you were to cut a true bulb in half, you would find a neatly packed next year's plant surrounded by the scale leaves—immature foliage, flower stems, possibly even flower buds in some.

The term "bulb" is one that we loosely apply to any plant with a swollen or thickened storage organ from which the stalk grows up and roots grow down. The sketches show the difference between a true bulb and a corm, a tuber, a rhizome, or a tuberous root. Actually the first four are all modified stems (not roots), whereas tuberous roots are true roots (not stems) with thickened sections somewhere along their length.

Nevertheless, all of these bulbs and bulblike structures have one characteristic in common: they are the food storage bins that the plant can draw on to start active growth after its season of dormancy. They are the reason that you let the foliage stay on the plant until it has ripened and dried naturally. Food for these reserves in the bulbs is manufactured in the leaves: the longer the leaves work the bigger the bulb, and consequently, next year's plant.

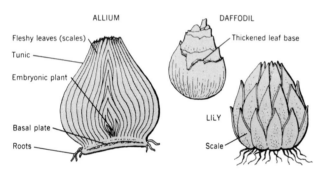

TRUE BULB. *Short underground stem (on solid basal plate) surrounded by fleshy leaves (scales) that protect, store food for use by embryonic plant. Outer scales dry, form papery covering (tunic). Daffodil scales are thickened bases of foliage leaves.*

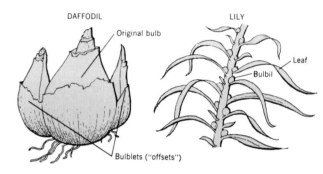

Bulblet (often called "offset"). The new bulb is formed from a lateral bud on the basal plate. The old bulb may die or, like daffodils, keep coming each year; it can be divided and replanted. Bulbils are small bulbs produced in axils of leaves, flower, stems.

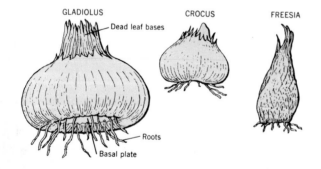

CORM. *Swollen underground portions of stem—usually broader than high—covered with one or more dead leaf bases; has basal plate. Food storage is in the solid tissue. New corms formed from axillary buds on top of old corm during growing season.*

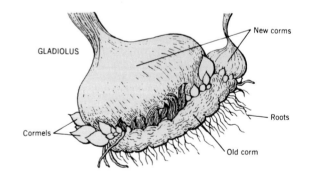

Cormel. While one to several big new corms are forming, smaller ones (cormels) are also being produced from the axillary buds on top of the old corm. The cormels will take two to three years to bloom, while the larger corms will blossom the following year.

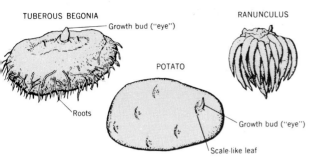

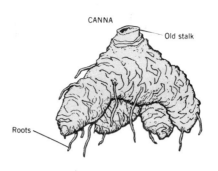

TUBER. *Short, fat, underground stem is for food storage; it is either flattened, rounded, or irregular. Does not creep like a rhizome. Usually knobby with growth buds (eyes)—each a scale-like leaf with bud in its axil. Divide large tubers like rhizomes for new plants.*

TUBEROUS ROOTS. *Actually roots (not stems), with thickened food storage structures. They do not bear growth buds in "tubers" but can be divided in the same way as rhizomes and tubers—cut sections with part of old stem base attached. Growth buds are in old stem.*

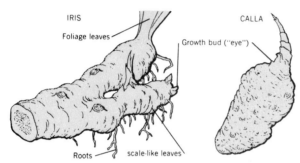

RHIZOME. *A thickened stem for food storage that grows horizontally along or under the surface of the soil. Foliage, roots, and flower stalks grow from buds on the rhizome. Cut sections of the rhizome with growth buds for new plants. Terms rootstock and rhizome are interchangeable.*

PLANTS LISTED ACCORDING TO TYPE OF "BULB"

True bulbs	Iris	Sternbergia	Freesia	Begonia
Allium	Ipheion uniflorum	Tigridia	Gladiolus	Caladium
Amaryllis belladonna	Lachenalia	Tulip	Ixia	Cyclamen
Camassia	Leucocoryne	Vallota	Sparaxis	Dahlia
Chionodoxa	Leucojum	Veltheimia	Tritonia	Eranthis
Crinum	Lilium	Zephyranthes	Tulbaghia	Gloriosa
Eucomis	Lycoris		Watsonia	Polianthes
Fritillaria	Milla	**Corm**		Ranunculus
Galanthus	Muscari	Acidanthera	**Rhizome**	Sinningia
Galtonia	Narcissus	Babiana	Achimenes	
Habranthus	Nerine	Brodiaea	Iris	**Tuberous roots**
Haemanthus	Ornithogalum	Calochortus	Oxalis	Agapanthus
Hippeastrum	Oxalis	Colchicum	Schizostylis	Bletilla
Hyacinth	Scilla	Crocus	Zantedeschia	Bulbinella
Hymenocallis	Sprekelia	Dierama	**Tuber**	Canna
		Erythronium	Anemone	Clivia

Growing Healthy Bulbs

. . . planting, care, container culture, pests, diseases

As you read about each bulb or bulblike plant in the encyclopedia chapter, you will find basic information related to that plant: its origin, whether it is hardy or tender, and what its basic cultural requirements are (light, soil, planting depth, spacing, watering, feeding, lifting and dividing, storing, etc.).

Here are some important general cultural points that apply to all kinds mentioned in this book, as, in fact, they do to most plants. (In the following text, the term "bulb" is used whether the plant is a corm, tuber, rhizome, tuberous root, or true bulb.)

GROWTH REQUIREMENTS

Bulbs are easy and fun to grow. Certainly from no other group of plants can you obtain a surer return, since the embryo flower is already present in the bulb when you buy it. But to transform ordinary looking brown bulbs into brilliant flowers year after year requires knowledge of their growth requirements.

Soil and Fertilizer. Throughout this book, under the heading of culture, you will read such terms as "good garden soil," "well prepared soil," "well drained soil," or "soil containing humus" so frequently as to become almost monotonous. The repetition is justified when you realize that soon after you plant it, a bulb starts putting out roots that will go down twice as deep (or more) as the depth of the bulb itself. (Some bulbs like lilies and amaryllis already have roots when you plant them.) To enable these roots to grow to their full depth, the soil should be porous well below the base of the bulb.

The ideal soil for most bulbs is one that is porous and drains well and yet still holds enough water for the roots. Such a soil generally contains some organic matter. If your soil is heavy clay and drains slowly or very sandy and does not hold water, it can be improved by adding about 30 per cent in volume of such organic soil amendments as peat moss, ground bark, "aged" sawdust, or buckwheat hulls. To do this, spread a 3 to 4-inch layer of one of the soil amendments over the bulb bed and work it in to a depth of 9 to 12 inches. Since the amendments listed above contain little or no nutrients, place a complete commercial fertilizer on the surface of the added material, and incorporate them together with the soil. Follow label directions for preplanting application.

If your garden soil contains adequate organic material, there is no need to add fertilizer at planting time. However, to replace nutrients used by the plants during a season's active growth and to build up the bulbs for the next year's bloom, apply complete fertilizer before and after flowering.

Phosphate fertilizers should always be used in the area of the intended root zone. Place superphosphate or bonemeal at the bottom of the planting trough and work it in prior to planting. In subsequent years, apply these phosphate fertilizers to the surface and cultivate it into the soil.

Manure can be incorporated for its nutrient and organic contributions. Manure usually supplies substantial quantities of phosphorus and potassium. To minimize conditions resulting from high soluble salt content, manure should never be used when its volume will exceed 10 per cent of the total soil mass.

Planting. For the most part, the sooner you plant bulbs after they become available, the better. There are a few exceptions: in warmer climates, such bulbs as daffodils and tulips are better held in cool storage until the warm weather is over. Lilies, which never are completely dormant, are especially sensitive to drying out and should be planted without delay. If it is impossible to plant lily bulbs immediately after receiving or digging them, store them in peat moss, sawdust, or vermiculite in a cool place.

A general rule for planting bulbs is to set them at a depth approximately three times their greatest diameter. Plant a little deeper in sandy soil, less deeply in heavy soils. If you are planting a large number of bulbs in one bed, it is often easier to excavate the entire area to the recommended depth, work fertilizer (if needed) into the bottom of the trench, set out the bulbs, and cover them all at one time. This way insures planting to a uniform depth—quite important when you are setting out bulbs in a precise, formal arrangement. For smaller plantings, the tools especially designed for planting bulbs are useful.

If you plan to combine bulbs and perennials in the same area, it is generally best to set out the surface plants first to avoid planting directly on top of the bulbs. But if it's more convenient to reverse the procedure, mark the location of each bulb with a small pile of sand. You can plant the ground cover in several days, or even weeks later, without fear of superimposing them on the bulbs.

Watering. When bulbs are growing actively, they need abundant moisture. Remember that the roots of the bulbs are located quite deep in the ground, and require more than casual surface watering. If the rains do not come soon after planting bulbs in the fall (in parts of the West, it is often late November, or even December or January before drenching rains arrive) the area should be watered thoroughly. Usually one good soaking is sufficient until the tops of the plants appear. After the bulbs have finished blooming, continue watering until the leaves naturally turn yellow. Good drainage is important.

TO TIDY UP the garden while bulb leaves ripen, pull leaves together, fold over, secure with rubber band.

Mulching. Mulches help prevent soil from drying out and crusting, from muddying plants during rains; they also discourage growth of weeds, and look neat. In hot dry climates, as in the Southwest, mulches are extremely helpful in keeping the soil cool during warm weather following planting. In cold-winter areas, mulches of straw, salt hay, evergreen boughs, and non-packing leaves are useful in preventing alternate freezing and thawing of the soil.

After-bloom care. Do not cut off the leaves of the bulb until they have become dry. The nourishment in the leaves must be returned to the bulb for the development of next year's bloom. Not only should you avoid cutting the leaves but also you should continue watering until the leaves turn yellow, thus indicating that they have completed their important assignment of storing food to carry the bulb through to the next season.

To make these unsightly clumps of sprawling leaves less conspicuous in the meanwhile, pull the leaves together, fold them over, and secure with a rubber band. Then set out some annuals to help camouflage the bound leaf clumps. The bulbs will benefit from water and fertilizer given to the annuals. When the foliage turns yellow, a light tug will remove it from the bulb.

If it is necessary to dig the bulbs before their foliage has matured, lift the clumps carefully so as to disturb the roots as little as possible and heel them into the ground somewhere else, where they can continue growing and ripening their foliage.

In digging bulbs or cultivating beds in which they are growing, be careful not to injure bulbs, since diseases and pests often enter bulbs through cuts or bruises. The best tool for digging bulbs is a spading fork; you are likely to slice through the bulbs with a spade. If you notice damaged bulbs, dust the injured sections with sulfur or a bulb dust.

Storing. Early spring bulbs and naturalized plantings should be left to their own devices. Other spring bulbs can be left alone or lifted from garden beds after blooming and ripening to make room for other plants. In cold weather climates summer blooming bulbs cannot take the cold of winter and must be dug up and stored properly until they can be planted again in the spring.

Dry bulbs for about a week in a dark ventilated spot. Then remove any clinging dirt; dust with fungicide powder to prevent rot. Place the bulbs in an unsealed paper bag or a nylon stocking with some dry peat moss to keep bulbs from touching one another. Store spring blooming bulbs at temperatures between 60° and 70°; summer blooming bulbs need lower temperatures, from 45° to 60°.

Propagation. Bulbs can be propagated either by seed or division. Commercial growers use both methods. When developing new varieties, they crossbreed existing varieties and plant the resulting seed, and select desirable offspring. Then they cut or divide the bulbs in order to maintain a particular color, form, or size. Division also yields a much quicker return; it usually takes two to three years for a seed to mature enough to produce a satisfactory bloom.

For fast, reliable results, you will probably want to increase your bulb collection by division, unless otherwise directed in the encyclopedia chapter. True bulbs grow larger each year until they reach a maximum size. At this point they form two or more smaller bulbs (also called bulblets or offsets) that can be broken off and replanted. Corms disappear at the end of each season but leave behind one or more new corms. You divide tubers, tuberous roots, and rhizomes by cutting into smaller pieces. When cutting them, include an eye or part of the stem base with each piece in order to produce a new plant.

BULBS IN CONTAINERS

You can enjoy a brilliant flower show at close range if you plant bulbs in containers. Then during the more unsightly stages—after planting when it is just a pot of dirt and after blooming while the leaves are ripening—you can move the container to a less conspicuous spot.

Most bulbs are easy to grow in containers. In the encyclopedia chapter you will find which ones are best adapted to container culture.

Some bulbs can be grown permanently in containers and will flower year after year with little more than an occasional repotting or refurbishing of the soil. Among these are achimenes, agapanthus, amaryllis, caladium, calla, canna, clivia, crinum, and haemanthus.

Many other bulbs, like crocus, daffodils, Dutch iris, freesias, hyacinths, scillas, and tulips, are usually grown in containers for one season (in colder sections, they are frequently forced for indoor bloom); after flowering, the bulbs are planted out in the garden for color in future years.

The medium most generally used for bulbs grown in containers is a loose, fibrous mixture containing equal parts of loam, coarse sand, and organic matter (peat moss, leaf mold, or ground bark). Whenever a bulb requires a special mixture, we have so specified in the section dealing with the culture of that bulb.

Use clean pots (the shallower kinds are more attractive and are suitable for most bulbs). Place a piece of broken crock, concave side down, over the drainage hole, then add the soil mixture. Set bulbs so that they almost touch each other, with the tips level with the surface of the soil. An 18-inch pot will take 15 to 18 bulbs (be sure to buy Number 1 bulbs). Plant smaller bulbs with the tips slightly under the surface. (Although deeper planting—three times the diameter of the bulb—is recommended for most bulbs set in the ground, you can plant more shallowly in containers if you protect the containers as directed below). Leave about an inch of space below the rim of the pot for watering. After thoroughly soaking the potted bulbs, place them in a cool, dark place for the duration of the rooting period. A shaded spot on the north side of the house or under a tree will keep soil in pots cool and prevent premature sprouting. Where winters are extremely warm, you will need further insulation to keep bulbs cool while root action begins.

You can either bury the pots in a trench or place them in a coldframe. For a few pots, a bushel basket or an apple box makes a convenient storage unit—or, in milder climates, you can build a temporary frame on top of the ground with boards or several courses of concrete blocks. Label pots well.

Cover the pots with 6 to 8 inches of moist peat moss, wood shavings, sawdust, or sand. Some gardeners place an inverted pot (of the same size) over the planted pot to protect future emerging shoots. If you cover the pots with soil, first place a layer of sand over the pots to keep them clean. In the coldest climates, provide extra protection by putting a thick layer of straw, evergreen boughs, or some boards on top.

After 8 or 10 weeks, lift a few pots and look for roots. Remove pots with well rooted bulbs; top growth may be showing, but it will be pale yellow or white from lack of light. As the plants are gradually exposed to full light the shoots will turn green.

Keep the plants evenly moist throughout active growth and until the leaves turn yellow naturally. When both foliage and soil are dry, you can tip the bulbs out of the pots and plant them in the garden. Bulbs that have been forced rarely bloom satisfactorily the second year.

Lilies are usually planted individually in containers. Place one bulb in a 5 or 7-inch pot, depending on the size of the bulb. Use deep pots; fill the pot 1/3 full with soil mixture, place the bulb with roots spread and pointing downward, and cover with about an inch of soil. Water thoroughly and place in a deep coldframe or a greenhouse that is heated (in colder climates) just enough to keep out frost. During the root forming period, keep the soil moderately moist. When the top growth appears, add more soil mixture and gradually fill the pot as the stems elongate. Leave 1 inch of space between the surface of the soil and the rim of the pot for watering. Move the pots onto a partially shaded terrace or patio during their blooming period.

When the foliage turns yellow, withhold water somewhat but do not let the soil become bone-dry, since lilies never go completely dormant. Repot the bulbs in late fall or early spring.

DISEASES AND PESTS

Sound, healthy bulbs set out in a well-cared-for garden have a good chance of growing into beautiful

FORCING: ANTICIPATE SPRING WITH BULBS

Bulbs are highly adaptable for forcing into bloom ahead of their outdoor schedule. By giving them a warm temperature earlier than nature would provide it, you can persuade bulbs to give you a taste of spring when it's still cold and bleak outdoors.

Most bulbs that are hardy outdoors are suitable for forcing. In order to force bulbs satisfactorily, you must start with top quality bulbs and control the temperature and light during the growing period. In effect, you simulate their subterranean springtime conditions. Bulbs cannot be forced to bloom a second year, but if allowed to ripen naturally and then planted in the outdoor garden, they will bloom in future years. Bulbs can be forced to bloom in several mediums beside the soil mixture described on page 10.

Water. Hyacinths can be grown in water alone if a special hyacinth glass (shaped like a large egg cup) is used. The bulb sits on top and the roots extend into the water below. Fill the glass with only enough water to touch the base of the bulb, refilling it to that level as the water evaporates. Some gardeners put a piece of charcoal in the water to keep it sweet.

Pebbles and water. Place a 2 or 2½-inch layer of clean pebbles in a bowl or dish 3 inches or more deep. Set the bulbs so that the lower half is under the pebbles, then fill the container with water until it is level with the base of the bulbs. Check the water level frequently for evaporation, adding more water if necessary. 'Paper White,' 'Soleil d'Or,' and 'Chinese Sacred Lilies' narcissus are among the reliable bulbs for growing this way. For best results, select large, firm, single-nosed bulbs.

Vermiculite. Soak the vermiculite thoroughly, squeeze out the excess moisture, and fill the bowl almost to the top, pressing down — but not too firmly, or roots will have a hard time pushing through. Form a depression in the vermiculite, position the first bulb, then place the remaining bulbs so that they support one another. Crocus make a cheerful display in small terra cotta bowls with round windows in the sides. As you fill the bowl with vermiculite, place a crocus corm at each of the eight side holes. Position a few corms at the top and cover them with a thin layer of vermiculite. In addition to the bulbs suggested for forcing in pebbles and water, hyacinths and early trumpet daffodils are good bulbs to grow in vermiculite.

After planting bulbs according to the methods above, place the containers in a dark cold place — as in a closet — where bulbs can produce roots. Rooting usually takes 10 to 13 weeks, depending on the kind of bulb. When a mass of roots has formed and the tips of the bulbs are an inch or two high, move the containers into full light in a cool room (between 50° and 60°). Keep the rooting medium evenly moist but not soggy wet.

THESE SPRING blooming bulbs were forced to bloom ahead of schedule: (from left to right) crocus peek out the windows of a pot filled with vermiculite; narcissus grow from a saucer of pebbles and water; hyacinth blooms in water.

plants comparatively free of troubles. But there are times when the provident gardener will want to know which diseases and pests affect bulbs, and how to prevent and control them.

It so happens that the very structure of bulbous plants, with their tissue connections to the old bulb and their close proximity to the soil, provide ideal conditions for the perpetuation of many types of disease and insects. A classic example is the virus of tulips, which produces brilliant colors and artistic markings on the blossoms. In the 17th century, tulips exhibiting this color break were considered to be a special strain and were highly valued. Although at that time nothing was known of their relationship to virus, it was proved that a flower pattern could be propagated from bulb to bulb, showing how easily diseases can be transferred by bulbs.

Rots caused by bacteria and fungus can also be transferred readily. The microscopic worms known as nematodes are carried with the bulbs and sometimes are so imbedded in the tissues that the only way to destroy them is to immerse the bulbs in hot water. Various species of the fungus *Botrytis,* which cause the most severe blighting of leaves and flowers, are also carried over on the bulb and affect the new emerging plant. It is best to destroy infested or diseased bulbs. Insects are also readily carried over with the bulbs: important examples are thrips, which cause severe damage to flowers, and the narcissus bulb fly.

Foliage and flower blights (or "fire"). This group of diseases is worldwide in distribution and quite destructive. The diseases are caused by similar, but distinct fungi, mostly species of *Botrytis.* Narcissus, lilies, and tulips are particularly susceptible.

The disease usually begins with a diseased bulb or with contaminated soil in which the fungus is living on the remains of an infected plant. As a new shoot pushes through the soil, it becomes infected, and under continued cool, moist conditions, powdery masses of spores are formed which can blow to other plants and initiate further infections. It is this highly infectious and disastrous stage that has resulted in the name "fire."

To reduce incidence of *Botrytis* diseases, plant bulbs in locations with good air circulation. Avoid especially low or shaded areas and massed planting.

To control, use a garden fungicide containing phaltan, captan (with a spreader-sticker for good sticking or wetting action), maneb, or ferbam weekly in wet, cool weather. Promptly remove and destroy diseased leaves and flowers to reduce the source of infection and spread of spores.

If bulbs are infected, dig them up and destroy them. Plant clean, healthy bulbs in a new, uninfected location.

Bulb rots. Several organisms cause rots in bulbs, but the most important and difficult to control are caused by specific types of the fungus *Fusarium.* This fungus thrives under high temperatures—the reason why sound appearing bulbs removed from cool soil often break down rapidly when stored at high temperatures. The fungi causing bulb rot not only carry over readily in bulbs but also remain in infested soil for several years. Bulbs that are particularly susceptible are dahlia, gladiolus, hyacinth, lily, and narcissus.

To control rots, start with bulbs that are as clean as possible; rotate crops as frequently as you can; harvest bulbs before the soil temperatures get too high; handle bulbs carefully during digging, sorting, cleaning, and storage, so as to avoid marring or damaging them; store in a shallow tray in well ventilated areas; remove and discard rotted bulbs as soon as noticed; and dip before planting in a fungicide containing benlate, captan or phaltan.

Pests. Aphids can be troublesome on many bulbs during warm or moist spring weather. Not only do they cause yellowing and twisting of leaves by sucking cell sap but also they spread virus diseases. The honeydew secretion exuded by aphids also furnishes nutriment for sooty molds and invites ants. First, try blasting the aphids off the bulb plants with water from the hose. If this won't work, spray with an insecticide.

Thrips are minute insects which cause gray or brown streaks on leaves, petals, and other tissues. They are particularly destructive on amaryllis, gladiolus, gloxinias, dahlias, and lilies. Control with spray containing nicotine sulfate, sevin, malathion, dibrom, or diazinon.

Mites infest bulbs of amaryllis, crocus, freesias, gladiolus, hyacinths, lilies, narcissus, and tulips, as well as some other bulbs. They often attack bulbs that are injured or diseased, extending the damage. Destroy badly infested bulbs. Control with sprays containing dibrom or diazinon.

Prevent damage by wireworms (which live in the soil and feed on dahlias, gladiolus, tuberous begonias, and other bulbs) by treating the bulbs and the soil in which they are planted with diazinon.

Snails and slugs can be controlled with baits, dusts, or sprays containing metaldehyde. To prevent early damage, apply controls when the leaves appear. Baits will last longer if protected from the weather with shingles or other shelter. Follow label directions carefully, especially if children and pets are around.

Pocket gophers, chipmunks, ground squirrels, and mice relish many bulbs (tulips are favorites); fortunately, they avoid narcissus because of their bitter taste. Surest methods of control include planting bulbs in raised beds, in wire baskets sunk in the ground, or in pots or other containers.

You may want to cover the planted area with chicken wire or netting to discourage animals and birds from uprooting the bulbs.

Ways to Use Bulbs

. . . versatility adds to their appeal

Almost any garden spot is suitable for some kind of flowering bulb: in beds or borders, in meadows or woods, by streams or in rock gardens. They are twice blessed, flourishing when planted in pots and one of the longest lasting cut flowers. It's been said that a garden without bulbs is only half a garden.

Some people are delighted most with a meadow of naturalized daffodils, where the art and craft of gardening is disguised. At the other extreme, Victorian gardeners found beauty in a formal scheme with each tulip exactly the same height and exactly in place.

The term "landscaping with bulbs" is misleading if it suggests that one must always plant with a lavish hand. Actually, most gardeners use bulbs as accents or highlights rather than as landscaping material. Very few home gardeners can plant bulbs by the thousands as in parks or estates, but this is by no means a disadvantage. Though it must be a thrill to look out upon your own acre of dancing daffodils, there's no question but that it's more challenging and fun to see what effects you can create with a few dozen or a handful of bulbs.

Whether you plant full sized or miniature bulbs or a combination of both, use them freely in borders, naturalized in ground covers, or under trees. Bulbs in borders are most effective when you place them in the foreground of a hedge, shrubbery border, fence, or other structure with at least 6 to 12 bulbs of one variety in each group.

The warm temperature and sunny skies of spring bring a procession of flowers with unbelievable rapidity. But the same factors that created this sudden spectacular show also hasten its conclusion. Therefore, for continuous garden color, you must plan carefully. For succession of color from daffodils, tulips, and other bulbs, select early, midseason, and late-blooming varieties. Fortunately bulbs don't limit their color to spring. Although most of us undoubtedly plant more of the spring flowering kinds, a great many bulbs bloom in summer and fall, and quite a few flower in the winter. So remember to combine bulbs with one another for a year-long show.

STATELY DARWIN TULIPS and bright snapdragons make superb garden companions. Edge this twosome with white sweet alyssum or blue, white, or yellow violas.

In Pots to Bring Indoors

You can bring a pot of blooming bulbs indoors if you disguise its utilitarian pot. In the fall, plant bulbs in a standard clay pot and follow directions for planting bulbs in containers on page 10. Then when the flowers start showing color in spring, slip them into a decorative indoor container and bring them inside.

It's fun to select a container that's just right—or a little surprising—for the flowers and their new location. In the kitchen, what better choice for big jaunty daffodils or tulips than an old-fashioned stoneware crock, a copper kettle, or a fish poacher? For crocus, grape hyacinths, or jonquils, why not use a milk pitcher or jam pot on the breakfast table?

If you cannot find a clay pot to fit a specific container, you can grow the bulbs in chicken wire baskets filled with soil. Make the baskets to fit the soup tureen, bean pot, charlotte mold, or whatever you would like to display the pot of bulbs in during their blooming period.

From 1-inch chicken wire, cut one piece to fit the inside walls of the container and another piece to fit the bottom of the container. With the first piece, form a cylinder and secure by bending ends together. To complete the basket, fasten cut ends of the bottom piece to the cylinder. Line the basket with heavy-duty aluminum foil and punch a few small holes in the bottom for drainage. Fill the basket with soil mix, plant bulbs in it, and treat it as any container of bulbs. When flowers start blooming, place the chicken wire container in the display container.

For both of these methods, it's best to select containers without holes in the bottom so that water draining from the clay pot or basket will not stain furniture. Potted bulbs brought indoors will keep fresh longer in cool or moderately heated rooms. Water enough to keep the soil moist; a surface mulch of pebbles, peat moss, sphagnum moss, or bark chips will help prevent drying out.

IRONSTONE SOUP TUREEN temporarily serves as a display container for a pot of white daffodils; at right, grape hyacinths grow in a 5-inch pot placed in a handcrafted pottery bowl during their indoor stay.

In Flower Arrangements

When bulbs blossom, many gardeners are content to enjoy them in the garden. But when cut and brought indoors, they make fine arrangements and bulbs are one of the longest lasting cut flowers. Cutting the flower stems does not harm the plants; in fact, the bulbs become stronger because energy is not wasted in allowing the flowers to mature and produce seeds. Do not, though, cut the leaves; these must remain to build up the bulbs for the next year.

When picking flowers, be sure to select fresh, newly opened blooms; also pick a few buds with color just beginning to show to add interest and extend the life of the arrangement. The best time to cut flowers is in the early morning or evening. Place stems immediately in deep water. To straighten stems and flower heads of tulips, iris, callas, and gladiolus, wrap bunches of 6 to 12 in newspaper and place the bundles upright in a container filled with water. Let them stand for several hours or overnight.

In general, bulbs seem to lend themselves best to low, open containers in which flowers stand freely and are uncrowded. Some of the most pleasing arrangements have only a few bulb flowers complemented with leaves and blooms of another flowering plant with contrasting texture. Tulips and heather are as interesting together in arrangements as they are in the garden.

In a radiating arrangement using daffodils or tulips, it is helpful to tie together (with inconspicuous twine or thread) two or three stems that will occupy the center of the arrangement. With this support they will stand upright and stay in place.

IN THE SIMPLE ARRANGEMENT above, tightly budded birch branch shows off the fine form of Dutch iris; in the long lasting arrangement below, 'King Alfred' daffodils are complemented by feathery Sprenger asparagus.

DIMINUTIVE ARRANGEMENT of yellow crocus, flowering plum, and geranium leaves.

In Combination with Other Plants

Bulbs can star as the central planting of a garden, but they are also an interesting foil for other plants. Since bulbs have a relatively short bloom period, it makes sense to combine them with annuals and flowering perennials for a continuous garden show. And because bulbs are without foliage for part of the year, it is important to set them among plants that cover the ground or fill your garden with flowers when the bulbs are leafless.

Daffodils and violas (a classic combination) will do great things for each other — and for your spirits — in the spring. The plants provide an eye-pleasing contrast of color and shape; low growing blue violas set off the strong upright form of the yellow daffodils. More practically, as the daffodils fade, the longer blooming violas soften the change and extend garden color. Both share the need for ample water throughout the growing season. Planting this combination under deciduous trees is ideal: the daffodils get practically full sun while developing in the spring, and the shade provided later on prevents the violas from drying out.

If you plan to plant ground covers over bulbs, be sure to mark the location of the bulbs so you can cultivate or hoe the planting bed without cutting through the bulbs or endangering the sprouts about to emerge. As the ground cover patches spread, they will help keep down weeds, maintain an even soil temperature, and decorate the area with their own foliage and flowers when the bulbs are out of bloom.

To help you enjoy the rewarding pastime of creating living, growing, color pictures with bulbs, we offer suggestions for combining bulbs during each of the four seasons. You can carry out the following planting schemes with many or with a few bulbs, in large or small gardens, or even in containers.

Spring color in filtered shade.

Interlocking drifts of three little bulbs — yellow winter aconite (Eranthis), white, green-tipped snowdrop (Galanthus), and blue Siberian squill (Scilla sibirica). In cold climates, gardeners plant these bulbs in grass for a flowery meadow effect and let them naturalize.

White anemone interplanted with purple or white violets. Let these naturalize, too.

Miniature, violet-blue, crested iris (I. cristata) at the base of dwarf pink or white azaleas.

Late blooming, lemon yellow, miniature daffodils and golden brodiaea (B. lutea) — especially charming under autumn flowering cherry (Prunus subhirtella 'Autumnalis').

Spring color in sunny locations

Islands of yellow trumpet daffodils in a sea of baby-blue-eyes (Nemophila) or blue forget-me-nots (Myosotis).

Blue carpet of grape hyacinths or Scilla sibirica under clear yellow forsythia.

Yellow daffodils, red tulips, and yellow doronicum — a combination for those who like brilliant color.

Charming carmine-and-white lady or candy tulips (Tulipa clusiana) with foamy white arabis or perennial candytuft (Iberis).

Orange tulips, golden yellow wallflowers, and orange fritillaria.

White, pink, or blue hyacinths under a dwarf pink flowering almond.

Gay, bright colored sparaxis and silvery gray Sedum spathulifolium — ideally adapted to sunny borders or to rock gardens in mild climates.

Summer and early fall color in filtered shade.

White lilies in a lush ground cover of glossy leafed plantain lily (Hosta).

Bellingham hybrid lilies among rhododendrons, lily-of-the-valley shrub (Pieris japonica), and tall ferns.

Tuberous begonias with a broad edging of blue lobelia.

White tuberoses (Polianthes) with coleus and ferns.

Summer and early fall color in sunny places.

White gladiolus and blue delphiniums (either the tall Pacific hybrids or the lower growing Belladonna — light blue, and Bellamosum — dark blue).

Bold masses of yellow and bronze dahlias with lemon yellow, medium-height marigolds in the foreground.

(Continued on page 18)

CYCLAMEN WITH FAIRY PRIMROSES

TUBEROUS BEGONIA WITH LOBELIA

NARCISSUS WITH VIOLETS

NARCISSUS UNDER BIRCHES

GLADIOLUS WITH CHARD, ENGLISH DAISIES

17

Dwarf cannas in masses of a single color edged with white petunias.

Flashy red and yellow tigridias in a carpet of blue lobelia.

White summer hyacinth *(Galtonia)* and violet-blue or coral petunias, or white or red annual phlox.

Blue agapanthus and yellow daylily or red and yellow poker plant *(Kniphofia)* — ideal for a wide border.

Orange-red *Tritonia crocata* and gray foliaged snow-in-summer *(Cerastium tomentosum)*.

Blue agapanthus and fragrant pink *Amaryllis belladonna* with a billowy edging of white petunias.

White zephyr lilies *(Zephyranthes)* and scarlet flowering *Kalanchoe blossfeldiana*.

Golden yellow *Sternbergia lutea* with gray-green hen-and-chickens *(Sempervivum tectorum)*.

Late fall and early winter color in light shade.

Pink hardy cyclamen *(C. neapolitanum)* and blue-purple lily turf *(Liriope muscari)*.

Autumn crocus *(Colchicum autumnale)* interplanted with spring flowering blue scillas and yellow doronicum under high branching deciduous trees.

Late fall and early winter color in sunny areas.

Lavender winter iris *(I. unguicularis)* under a canopy of fragrant, yellow flowering wintersweet *(Chimonanthus praecox)*. Despite their common names, both of these plants bloom in late fall in mild winter areas.

Blue, autumn flowering crocus *(C. speciosus)* in a ground cover of green or woolly gray thyme.

Winter color.

Even in the coldest winter you can have colorful blooms between the last autumn flowering crocus or hardy cyclamen and the first snowdrop or chionodoxa of spring if you grow bulbs in pots in a sunny window or greenhouse.

There are exotic hybrid amaryllis, florists' cyclamen (usually in bloom by Christmas), glamorous gloxinias, richly colored clivias, fragrant freesias, gay sparaxis, and the unusual lachenalia. Then there are the bunch-flowered or Polyanthus narcissus such as 'Paper White' and 'Soleil d'Or,' hyacinths, early flowering single tulips, crocuses, and *Iris reticulata* to brighten a gloomy winter day.

NATURALIZING: FOLLOW NATURE'S EXAMPLE

Naturalized plantings are informal naturalistic arrangements that require minimum care. It's a garden technique where bulbs are planted in loose drifts as if growing wild, and it's based on an appreciation of nature's patterns but not slavish imitation of them. To do this, limit the species or varieties in one area and avoid planting in anything approaching a regular pattern.

To naturalize densely but unevenly, strew handfuls of bulbs in long sweeping motions so they fall in elongated patterns and with greater density at one end of each drift than at the other, as if the wind had had a hand in the planting. It's important to plant the bulbs far enough apart to leave room for them to grow larger and increase their yield of flowers.

Naturalized plantings flourish in open woodland areas where the trees are spaced widely enough apart to allow the plants a few hours of sun each day, or on sunny slopes, or along winding paths, or about the outskirts of a garden.

One of the great joys of naturalized bulbs is that they need little care. Certainly all benefit from an annual application of a complete fertilizer right before the blooming period. When the number and size of flowers lessens, it's time to dig up, separate, and replant.

CHILDREN CELEBRATE the arrival of spring in an open meadow where naturalized daffodils grow.

In Containers on Patios

Bulbs are especially successful when displayed in containers on a patio or deck. You need not worry about fading foliage or short blooming periods as you do when bulbs are planted in the ground. The mobility provided by the containers gives you color where you want it on your patio. Best of all, you can enjoy a wide variety, since it takes only a dozen or less of some kinds of bulbs to make an effective showing in a container. Patio growing is best where extremes of heat and cold do not persist.

If you have large windows or doors that face toward the patio, containers of bulbs placed close to the glass seem almost a part of the room. The indoors and outdoors seem to blend together. A container or two of bulbs can be brought inside, as well, for an even more effective blending of the two areas.

If you select species and varieties according to their bloom periods, you can enjoy a steady succession of bulb color throughout the year. Or rotate containers of bulbs with other container plants so your stage is always full of blooming plants.

HANGING TUBEROUS BEGONIAS

TULIPS MOVED CLOSE-UP DURING BLOOM

TULIPS NEAR A WINDOW TO VIEW FROM INDOORS

Miniatures

. . . the little children of the bulb world

Although miniature bulbs aren't fragile, you still feel like babying them along.

There's no set rule about what constitutes a miniature bulb, but it's generally considered in that class if the stems are no higher than 8 inches and flowers are correspondingly small. The most miniature of the miniatures, *Narcissus* 'Minimus,' has a bulb about the size of a tiny pea; the blossom hardly covers a five-year-old's fingernail, and the stems are short enough to arrange in a thimble.

Many of the most appealing miniature bulbs are species (wild forms); some may be more difficult to grow under garden conditions, particularly in mild winter climates, than the popular hybrid varieties. The little wild daffodils, for instance, generally reproduce by seed rather than division and are short-lived compared to many of the large flowered varieties, whose bulbs proliferate and bloom year after year. Yet miniature bulbs are relatively inexpensive, and gardeners who have grown these fascinating plants don't hesitate to buy new bulbs each year.

In cold winter areas, it's definitely worth planting miniature wildlings such as species crocus, daffodils, glory-of-the-snow, Siberian squill, various species tulips, and winter aconite in rock gardens and walls, between paving stones, in the foreground of borders, and under high branching trees.

But in warmer regions—except for a few kinds such as grape hyacinth and lady tulip—the best and safest way to grow miniature bulbs is in containers. There you can provide the right soil, perfect drainage, cool temperatures during the rooting period, and shade from hot sun while flowers bloom. You can dry the bulbs out properly after bloom and protect the bulbs from rodents and other pests. Best of all, you can bring your miniatures into the house in late winter or early spring and enjoy their exquisite flowers at close range.

Plant miniature bulbs as soon as possible after you buy them. If you can't plant them immediately, store them in aerated bags in a cool place, such as the bottom of the refrigerator (about 42°). This is especially important in warmer areas.

Choose correspondingly small containers. If you use a shallow pot, save root space by covering the drainage hole with a piece of fine wire or plastic screen instead of the usual piece of broken crock. Little bulbs, like most of their large counterparts, grow best in a light, fast-draining, sandy loam. Plant the bulbs with tips slightly under the surface of the soil. Thoroughly soak the container, place in a flat or box in a cool shaded spot, and cover with 2 to 3 inches of mulch. Keep covered and moist until bulbs form roots.

After the roots form, usually in six to eight weeks, remove the mulch and expose the plants to full light but not to direct sun. As leaves elongate, gradually expose plants to more sunlight. Keep the soil moist during bloom and until flowers fade and leaves start to turn yellow. After the leaves have died down naturally, let the bulbs dry out in the soil.

TINIEST OF ALL trumpet daffodils, Narcissus *'Minimus' is a perfect miniature replica of large trumpets.*

DWARF DAFFODIL (Narcissus lobularis), only 5 to 7 inches tall, has a perky lemon yellow flower.

AZURE BLUE grape hyacinth (Muscari armeniacum) has neat upright leaves, grows to 6 inches tall.

IT'S FUN to grow the miniature species tulips, such as this Tulipa clusiana, in a decorative charlotte mold.

JAUNTY YELLOW hoop petticoat daffodil grows only 4 to 6 inches tall, is also a good rock garden subject.

AMARYLLIS BELLADONNA   ANEMONE

ANEMONE

Encyclopedia of Bulbs

In this encyclopedia you will find bulbs from A (Achimenes) to Z (Zephyranthes). Among these are many well known favorites like anemone, crocus, freesia, ranunculus, and tigridia. But we hope that you will come across some strangers — bulbs with such odd-sounding names as acidanthera, babiana, leucocoryne, sternbergia — that you would like to become acquainted with.

Achimenes

Rhizome. Tender.

If you have been successful in growing African violets or gloxinias, you should have no trouble with achimenes.

From tiny, cone-like rhizomes grow slender stems clothed with roundish, crisp, bright to dark green, hairy leaves. Flower buds form in axils of leaves — usually singly or in pairs. Flaring tubular flowers, in pink, blue, orchid, lavender, and purple vary in size according to kind. Plants grow 12 to 24 inches high, some trailing in habit.

Use: In pots or hanging baskets or in pots plunged in semi-shaded beds.

Culture: Start rhizomes between January and April (the latter month is preferred in colder sections). Plant them ½ to 1 inch deep in a mixture of moist peat moss and sand. Keep them in a warm, lightly shaded location where temperatures don't go below 60°.

Maintain even moisture but be careful not to overwater, since rhizomes may rot. After growth starts, increase watering slightly and give plants more light, but never expose them to hot direct sunlight. Warm, filtered shade suits them ideally.

When plants are 3 inches high, transplant them to a 6 or 7-inch fern pot; place 6 to 12 rhizomes to a pot. Use a loose potting mixture containing equal parts of peat moss, sand or perlite, and leaf mold.

After flower buds show, fertilize once a month with a liquid fertilizer. At this time you may move the plants to the lathhouse or to a covered patio where they are protected from wind. In such a situation, they will give a spectacular flower show right through the summer.

In cold-winter climates, achimenes are usually grown in greenhouses, as house plants, or in window boxes and pots for summer bloom.

Any portion of the leaf, stem, or rhizome of achimenes will root readily when broken off and planted. And the rhizomes themselves multiply at an incredible rate during a season. In the fall, dry and cure achimenes rhizomes just as you do begonia tubers. Store them in pots of soil in a cool, dry place in the winter; remove soil and repot in the spring.

Acidanthera

Corm. Tender.

First discovered in Tanganyika in the late 1800s, this plant is sometimes described as halfway between gladiolus and ixia. An outstanding characteristic of acidanthera is its drooping long-tubular flowers, flared at the top.

A. bicolor has fragrant, creamy white 2-inch-wide, 4 to 5-inch-long flowers blotched with dark chocolate brown; they are carried in loose, somewhat arching, spike-like clusters on 15 to 18-inch stems. Leaves also resemble those of gladiolus but are smaller. *A. bicolor murieliae* has heavily scented flowers of the same form and coloring as the species but is slightly taller.

Use: First and foremost cut flowers, acidantheras are valued particularly for their fragrance and long lasting qualities.

Culture: Plant in spring in a sunny, well-drained garden bed. In colder areas, start very early indoors. Plant corms 3 to 4 inches deep. Large acidantheras such as *A. b. murieliae* may be set 6 inches apart — smaller ones, such as *A. bicolor,* 4 inches apart. For a succession of bloom, make several plantings two to three weeks apart. After the first frost, lift the corms and dry them immediately (to prevent a fungus which causes rot) and store in dry peat moss, sand, or vermiculite in a cool, dry place.

RUFFLED DOUBLE PICOTEE BEGONIA

RUFFLED DOUBLE BEGONIAS UNDER FERNS

ROSE FORM PICOTEE BEGONIA

RUFFLED DOUBLE BEGONIA

ROSE FORM BEGONIA

CLIVIA

CANNA

BULBINELLA

25

Agapanthus

Tuberous rootstock.
Semi-hardy.

Now available in several
species and varieties, both
evergreen and deciduous,
and in heights varying
from 1 to 5 feet, these
South African plants have become standbys for summer color in mild climates. Both evergreen and deciduous agapanthus are hardy in western Oregon
and Washington. In cold winters, the leaves of evergreen kinds freeze to the ground, but the plants
recover before the growing season is over. In the
East and Midwest, agapanthus can be grown in pots
or tubs, although blooming may be uncertain.

Outstanding characteristics are the rich green,
strap-shaped leaves and straight, sturdy stems topped
with full clusters of funnel-shaped flowers in shades
of blue, purple, or white.

Following are the best known evergreen species
and varieties: *A. africanus* (*A. umbellatus*). African
lily—better known as, but erroneously called, lily-of-
the-Nile (it actually grows wild in the mountains of
the Cape of Good Hope); attractive clusters of 20 to
50 blue flowers on 3-foot stems. Its horticultural varieties include the following: 'Albidus,' with white
blooms; 'Mooreanus,' grass-like leaves, dark blue
flowers on 2-foot stems (it is hardier—in not too
severe climates it may live over outdoors with mulching); and 'Mooreanus Minor,' a smaller edition of
the foregoing variety.

A. orientalis is a larger and more robust species
that is often confused with *A. africanus*. It makes
large, full clumps of evergreen leaves and sends up
majestic 4-foot stems terminating in clusters with as
many as 100 flowers. It is available in a magnificent
white variety, as well as in a dwarf white form.

A. 'Rancho Dwarf.' Clusters of white flowers top
1½ to 2-foot tall stalks. The evergreen foliage clump
grows 1 to 1½ feet tall.

A. 'Peter Pan.' This outstanding free-blooming
dwarf variety has clustered blue flowers on top of
1 to 1½-inch stems. The foliage clumps are 8 to 12
inches tall.

Use: In borders, large agapanthus are impressive by
themselves or with other plants. Daylily, belladonna lily, and larger summer-blooming true lilies
enhance and are enhanced by the agapanthus' vi-
brant blues and shining white.

Agapanthus are superb container plants; they
actually seem to thrive in restricted space, flowering
more heavily as their roots become crowded.

As cut flowers, agapanthus have few peers; they
have crisp form, last well, and are easy to arrange.

Florists sometimes remove the individual flowers
from the clusters and combine them with other flowers in bridal bouquets.

Culture: In temperate climates, agapanthus is a sun-
lover, but too-hot or reflected sun may burn the
leaves. In warm, dry interior areas, it definitely needs
light shade. It grows best in a rich sandy loam.

Agapanthus seems to resent being divided too frequently. After about five or six years, clumps do get
overgrown and flowers are not as large as they once
were. Then it's time to divide. Spade up the clump,
shake off excess soil, separate the tuberous rootstocks, cut back leaves halfway, and replant. Divide
evergreen forms in spring or fall; divide the deciduous kinds in the fall. In the East and Midwest, agapanthus in borders must be dug and stored over the
winter. Agapanthus grows easily from seed sown in
the spring, but it takes two to three years to flower.

Allium

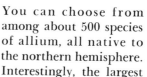

(Ornamental allium)
Bulb. Hardy.

You can choose from
among about 500 species
of allium, all native to
the northern hemisphere.
Interestingly, the largest
number of species in the New World are ornamentals
and are native to the mountains of the West, extending into central Mexico. Allium is also well suited to
the Pacific Northwest. Few species occur in the East.

No doubt the use of alliums in gardens has lagged
because so many gardeners assume that all ornamental kinds have the same odor as the familiar
edible alliums—garlic or onions. Actually, the odor
of the ornamentals offends only when the foliage is
bruised; it is not noticeable while their stems are in
water. Most of the flowers are odorless; a few are
fragrant. The fact is that any potential fault in many
of these plants is more than offset by beautiful flowers in shades of pink, rose, violet, red, blue, white,
and brilliant yellow. Alliums are striking in flower
arrangements, and few cut flowers last longer.

Ornamental alliums bear their flowers in compact
or loose roundish clusters at the ends of leafless stems.
They bloom throughout a longer season than any
other bulbs. Leaves usually grow from the ground.
Some alliums grow low, some grow tall, and some
giants stretch up to the height of a man.

A. albopilosum. Stars of Persia. This is a distinct
and handsome plant with an extremely large cluster

CHIONODOXA

CYCLAMEN

DUTCH CROCUS

DUTCH CROCUS

BABIANA STRICTA RUBROCYANEA

27

— as much as 1 foot in diameter — of lavender to deep lilac, star-like flowers with a metallic sheen. Stems are 12 to 15 inches tall, leaves grow to 18 inches in length and are white-hairy beneath. When dry, the flower cluster, with individual blooms still rigid and intact, makes a beautiful ornament.

A. caeruleum (A. azureum). Blue allium. True blue flowers are borne in rounded compact clusters on 1-foot-high stalks. Narrow, three-angled leaves grow 6 to 12 inches long. The plant blooms in June and is a wonderful companion for *A. moly.*

A. giganteum. Giant allium. Well named, this flower has stalks up to 5 feet tall. Bright lilac flowers in dense clusters bloom in July. The six to nine blue-green leaves are 1½ feet long and 2 inches wide.

A. karataviense. Turkestan allium. A unique and beautiful species, this one is characterized by a large, dense, round cluster of flowers varying in color from pinkish to beige to reddish lilac. Distinctive re-curving, blue-green leaves 2 to 5 inches across, of substantial texture, lie close to the ground.

A. moly. Golden garlic. Many bright, shining yellow flowers in open clusters top 1 to 1½-foot-high stalks from June to July. The flat leaves, up to 1½ inches wide, are almost as long as the flower stalks. This species naturalizes readily but is not permanent in cold climates.

A. neapolitanum. Spreading clusters of large white flowers, later becoming papery in texture, appear on 12-inch stems. Leaves are 1 inch wide and shorter than the flower stem. These plants are grown commercially in greenhouses as cut flowers and make splendid pot plants (indoors in colder climates). They bloom in May. A larger, slightly earlier blooming form of the variety 'Grandiflorum,' called 'Cowanii,' is said to be superior in all respects.

A. oreophilum. (A. ostrowskianum). This allium bears large loose clusters of rose-colored flowers in June on 8 to 12-inch stalks; each plant has two or three narrow, somewhat limp, gray-green leaves. There is a selected form, called 'Zwanenburg,' with deep carmine red flowers. It is recommended highly as a plant for rock gardens and cutting.

A. triquetrum. Here is one of the few shade-loving alliums. Triangular 1 to 1½-foot stems bear clusters of white, green-striped, nodding bells that bloom from late spring to early summer. Bright green leaves, attractive for a number of months, make a lush ground cover.

Use: Low-growing alliums are attractive as edgings for borders, in rock gardens, and in pots. The larger ones can be spectacular massed in borders. One of the most effective ways to use alliums is to let them naturalize under deciduous trees, on slopes, or along creek banks where they can grow like wild flowers.

Culture: Most of the alliums are hardy, sun-loving plants of easy culture. Although they will grow in most soils, they thrive in a rich, deep, well-drained, sandy loam. The plants need water during growth.

Set out bulbs in fall. Cover larger bulbs with about 4 inches of soil, smaller ones with 2 to 3 inches. Let bulbs remain undisturbed for several years or until they become crowded; then lift, separate, and replant as soon as leaves die down. Bulbs require very dry summer conditions.

Amaryllis, see *Hippeastrum.*

Amaryllis Belladonna

(Brunsvigia rosea,
Naked lady)
Bulb. Hardy to zero.

The belladonna lily (formerly called *Brunsvigia rosea*) has bulbs that seem practically indestructible. Nurserymen who have plowed, disked, and harrowed old field plantings find it coming up in the new plantings, whether it be roses, fruit trees, or ornamental shrubs.

During fall and winter, all you'll see are bold clumps of many strap-shaped leaves that spread 2 to 3 feet. These die down in early summer and are replaced in late summer or early fall by 2 to 3-foot-high, leafless, reddish brown stalks topped with trumpet-shaped, rosy pink, fragrant flowers.

Use: Because of its long leafless flower stems, it is best to plant belladonna lily among lower growing perennials that will make up for its lack of foliage. Blue agapanthus and pink belladonna lilies are a classic combination.

Culture: Plant in sun in almost any well-drained soil. Start with a bulb 2 inches to 6 inches in diameter and plant in fall or early winter. Set the bulbs with the tops even with, or slightly above, the level of the ground. Bulbs should be planted 6 inches deep in western Oregon and Washington. In the East and Midwest, grow as a pot plant for the house.

Belladonna lily is apparently immune to pests and diseases and thrives in the poorest soils under the driest conditions in the West.

These bulbs are shy blooming in western Oregon and Washington, although in unusually warm dry summers they produce splendid flowers. In these areas, always plant belladonna lilies in a southern exposure, preferably against a south wall.

Leave bulbs undisturbed for as long as possible; they seldom suffer from being crowded by numerous progeny. Move plants only in the season just after blooming; otherwise, you may have to wait years for your belladonna lilies to produce flowers.

Anemone

(Windflower)
Tuber.
Hardy or semi-hardy.

Two main groups of tuberous rooted anemones grow: the small, hardy kinds native to open woodlands, alpine slopes, or chalky downs (in England and on the continent); and the large, half-hardy, flamboyant anemones from southern Europe. Leaves of anemones are bright green, finely divided, and usually appear in basal tufts. The showy, spring-blooming flowers of both kinds grow singly on stems varying in height from 6 to 14 inches.

A. apennina. A hardy native of Italy's Apennine Mountains, this alpine plant produces sky blue blooms on 9-inch stems in March and April; it is also available in white and pink varieties. It grows in the dappled shade of woods in southern Europe and has also naturalized in English woodlands. It is a rock garden favorite in colder climates.

A. blanda. This species from mountains of Greece and Asia Minor is often confused with *A. apennina,* from which it differs in these respects: flowers are deeper blue, leaves are slightly smaller and less finely cut, flowers are borne on slightly shorter stems a little earlier than *A. apennina,* and the plant grows best in full sun. Other varieties are pink or white.

A. coronaria. The most commonly grown, large-flowered, tuberous anemone, this species has big poppy-like flowers in red, blue, violet, and white, with blue stamens. The poppy anemone is one of the parents of popular strains that are commonly planted in mild-climate gardens and are extensively grown in greenhouses for the florist cut flower trade.

The de Caen strain has single flowers in mixed colors. St. Brigid anemones are a popular strain of semi-doubles available in mixed colors. The beautiful St. Bavo strain comes in an exceptionally fine range of colors, unusual for anemones, that includes soft pink.

Use: In small gardens, concentrate clumps of small hardy anemones in rock gardens, in the foreground of borders, or at the base of flowering shrubs or trees. In larger gardens, the ideal way to grow these anemones is in woodland or meadow situations where they eventually form starry flowered mats of clear blue, pink, or white. In warmer, drier climates where small hardy anemones are not well adapted, the best way to grow them is in containers.

The large poppy anemones make brilliant splashes of spring color in pots or borders and are superior cut flowers.

Culture: Plant all anemones in perfectly drained, thoroughly prepared soil containing equal parts of loam, coarse sand, and humus (peat moss, leaf mold, or ground bark). Set out the small hardy anemones in fall, about an inch deep and 8 inches apart. Where conditions are favorable, these bulbs increase with little attention other than the application of a mulch of humus after the leaves have died down.

Plant the large poppy anemones in October or November in mild-winter areas, setting the tubers 1 to 2 inches deep and 8 to 12 inches apart. Place tubers with the rounded side facing upward and the bristly-looking top side facing downward.

Some gardeners in warmer climates soak the hard tubers in lukewarm water for a few hours before planting; in more humid areas, as in the Northwest, this is neither necessary nor desirable. Most gardeners find that it is better to plant new tubers of large flowered anemones each year than it is to lift and replant old ones, which rarely do well the second year. Anemones can also be grown from seed in early summer; they will bloom the following spring.

In the Midwest and East, large flowered anemones may be planted outside in spring after frosts. They often perform poorly, though, because of the rapid advance of hot weather later in spring.

Babiana

Corm. Tender.

Here is a plant commonly called "baboon flower" because in its native South Africa it is reported that the baboons eat the corms. In May or June it bears spikes of three or more freesia-like flowers (some species are fragrant) in blue, red, or cream, depending on the species. The hairy, sword-like leaves are strongly ribbed.

B. plicata grows to 6 inches or less high, the narrow leaves exceeding the flower spike. The lavender flowers with white markings smell like carnations.

B. stricta is taller (to 1 foot high), and the broader leaves are only half as high as the flower stems. The 1-inch-long flowers are royal blue, sometimes paler, with markings on the lower lip. Variety 'Rubrocyanea' grows only 5 to 6 inches high, the upper half of the flower blue, the lower red.

(Continued on page 31)

FORMAL DECORATIVE DAHLIA   CACTUS DAHLIA

FORMAL DECORATIVE DAHLIA

SEMI-CACTUS DAHLIA

(Continued from page 29)

Use: Effective plants for border edgings and along paths, in rock gardens, and in pots in colder climates where they are too tender to plant in the ground.

Culture: In milder sections, including western Oregon and Washington, plant corms 3 or 4 inches deep in November. Provide well drained soil in sun or very light shade. Plant outdoors in spring in severe climates. Set corms 4 inches deep and 2 or 3 inches apart; for a pleasing effect, plant a dozen or more in a group. Since most kinds of babiana grow wild in humid sections of the South African Cape, they need ample water while they are in active growth. Reduce watering after the leaves start to turn yellow. In extremely cold areas, lift and store the corms as you would gladiolus and replant in the spring.

Begonia

(Tuberous begonia)
Tuber. Tender.

When well grown, tuberous begonias can be the crowning glory of a garden in summer and early fall. Hybridists have developed an incredible number of different flower forms in an array of jewel-like colors. Not only do you find primary red and yellow but also practically every gradation—from pastel pinks to salmon, orange, apricot, soft yellow, and white. Plants are upright or pendulous; the upright form is *B. tuberhybrida*; the pendulous form is *B. t.* 'Pendula.'

Use: Tuberous begonias perform excellently in filtered light under high branching trees; on the east or north side of walls, fences, houses, or patios; and under roofs covered with lath, shade cloth, polyethylene, or a rigid plastic material that produces subdued light.

Fortunately, such environments provide ideal conditions for plants that combine well with tuberous begonias: shrubs such as azalea, camellia, leucothoe, lily-of-the-valley shrub *(Pieris)*, rhododendron, and skimmia; perennials such as campanula—especially the low-growing *C. elatines garganica, C. poscharskyana, C. portenschlagiana*; hellebores, primroses, and London pride *(Saxifraga umbrosa)*, and, of course, ferns. Among annuals, lobelia is unsurpassed as an edging for a bed of upright tuberous begonias, and trailing lobelia makes a graceful drapery over the edge of a basket or pot holding a pendulous begonia.

If your soil is not suitable for tuberous begonias, consider growing them in raised beds in which you can provide a made-to-order soil medium and perfect drainage.

Beautiful begonias can also be grown in pots or boxes. Many specialists prefer to grow begonias in cedar or redwood containers rather than in clay pots, since wood holds moisture better.

Culture: As indicated above, tuberous begonias prefer subdued light, not complete shade. In too much shade, plants get leggy and bloom sparsely. Strong wind is damaging to begonias; plant them on the lee side of larger plants or structures; but see to it that there is good air circulation to prevent development of mildew.

You can start tuberous begonias from seed, tubers, or cuttings. Later in spring, you can buy seedlings in flats.

• The seed mediums for tuberous begonias should be light, spongy, porous yet moisture-retentive. A leading grower of tuberous begonias uses only partially rotted, hardwood leaf mold. But in areas where leaf mold is difficult to obtain you can use ground bark, sphagnum moss, composted sawdust, peat moss, or vermiculite.

1. If you use leaf mold, ground bark, peat moss, or sphagnum moss, rub it through a ½-inch wire mesh screen. 2. Place a ½-inch layer of the coarse material (remaining in the sifter) over the bottom of a 3-inch-deep nursery flat or similar container. 3. Over this coarse material, spread a ½-inch layer of the finer screened medium. Sow the seed on top of this last layer.

Firm the surface lightly and moisten thoroughly with a fine spray. Some begonia growers use only distilled water until four weeks after the seedlings appear. Lightly dust seed with a hormone preparation and broadcast it thinly and evenly over the surface of the moist seed medium. Do not press the seed in or cover it. Place a sheet of glass over the seed flat and on top of this put a sheet of paper to exclude light.

A minimum temperature of 74°, maintained both below and on top of the seed container, is considered ideal. Germination should occur within eight days.

To maintain proper moisture content throughout the germinating period, check the seed container every other day. Remove the paper when you see signs that the seed coats are splitting—this will take place before evidence of green cotyledon leaves. Admit air by placing a matchstick between the glass and the edge of the flat. Remove the glass completely within a week to 10 days after germination. Keep seedlings evenly moist and give them enough light and air to keep them growing actively. A mild solution of fish emulsion (⅓ the recommended strength) applied once every two weeks will encourage vigorous growth.

About eight weeks after sowing seed, the seedlings will be ready to transplant into another flat. Fill this flat with the same material as for seeds but do not screen it. Continue feeding transplants at the same

SINGLE DAHLIA   FREESIA

rate and dilution as above. Plants started from seed in January or February will be ready for planting or potting in May or June.

• Start tubers about six to eight weeks before setting outdoors (after frosts). In mild winter climates, plants are started in January or February; in the Midwest and East in late March or April.

After pink buds show, set tubers in flats of coarse leaf mold or ground bark; allow sufficient space between tubers for full root development. Cover them with ½ inch of leaf mold or bark to encourage formation of roots on all surfaces of the tuber. Keep the rooting medium *evenly moist,* not soggy wet. Place the flat in a well-lighted area but out of direct sun—where the temperature remains between 65° and 75°. When tubers have produced two leaves and the weather has warmed, pot up the plants or set them out in the garden.

• You can grow tuberous begonias from cuttings made from shoots emerging from tubers started in flats. When stems have two leaves of equal size, cut off surplus shoots close to the base of the tuber below the basal ring—some shoots may already have produced roots. Leave one shoot on the tuber to continue growth.

Insert cuttings in a mixture of ½ sand and ½ leaf mold or in peat moss or ground bark. Cover the flat with plastic (6 to 8 inches above the cuttings) to hold in moisture and keep it heavily shaded for the first two weeks. When they are well rooted, place cuttings in pots in which they will bloom.

• Planting times vary according to climate. The general rule is to plant after the last frosts. Further variations are determined by local climatic conditions. In cool, moist, coastal sections, such as the Puget Sound and Northwest coastal area, it doesn't pay to set out tuberous begonias until the weather warms up—often as late as June. In inland sections where hot, dry winds start blowing in late spring, it's a good idea to set out tuberous begonias as soon as the weather permits so that plants may become established before it gets extremely hot. In such frost-free areas as the Southern California coast, you can set out tuberous begonias in March or early April. April and May are favored times in the central and northern sections of California.

In severe-winter climates of the East and Midwest, the best time to set out tuberous begonias is after you've planted tomatoes. It is difficult to grow tuberous begonias in the Southeast.

Since leaves and flowers of tuberous begonias always face in the same direction, set the plants so that the tips of the leaves face the front of the bed.

Although begonia specialists differ on specific ingredients, all agree that a planting or potting mixture for tuberous begonias should contain at least one-half organic matter—leaf mold, peat moss, ground bark, or compost. There are a few special-

ists who advocate using 100 per cent organic matter. A typical mixture includes ⅓ peat moss or ground bark, ⅓ leaf mold, and ⅓ sand. The idea is to provide a growing medium that will remain moist but allow water to drain through readily.

In potting tuberous begonias, allow 3 inches between the tuber and the side of the pot: for instance, place a 2-inch tuber in an 8-inch pot. Set the tuber so that the top is even with the surface of the soil.

When planting tuberous begonias outdoors, mix existing soil with ⅓ leaf mold, peat moss, or ground bark, and ⅓ coarse sand. If you use manure, be sure it is well rotted, thoroughly work it in a month before planting, and water the prepared bed several times. Barely cover the root ball with soil when you set it in the bed; and take care not to pile soil up around the plant stalk.

• Start feeding plants grown from tubers as soon as they are well established. Begin feeding seedlings, which have no tuber from which to draw upon for food, when they are a few inches high. You can tell when a begonia plant needs food by observing its leaves. Leaves that are light green and cupped upward signal that the plant requires feeding. Crisp dark green leaves that crimp downward indicate a well nourished plant.

In feeding tuberous begonias, the amount of fertilizer you use and the number of times you apply it are more important than the type you use. Any good complete fertilizer applied at regular intervals—these may vary from one a week to once every three weeks—will give satisfactory results. Stop feeding in September or six weeks before killing frosts.

• Begonias need ample moisture—especially atmospheric humidity—but too much water is not good for them, either. Overwatering can produce rot, molds, and a stagnant soil condition. In hot, dry climates, it is usually necessary to water tuberous begonias daily with an overhead sprinkler (or install a humidifying device) to cool and moisten the air. Water carefully, though, for too much overhead water on large, heavy flowered begonias weighs down the blooms and may cause stems to break off.

In the coastal fog belt, it is not necessary to artificially dampen the leaves of begonias and cool the air except on occasional hot days; in such areas, growers prefer to surface irrigate, thus reducing occurrence of mildew.

• In mild areas, allow tuberous begonias to continue growing into November (or until frosts) so that the tubers can store up as much food as possible. (In cold climates, gardeners sometimes lift plants before frost, pot them up, and place them in a light window where they may continue to bloom for a month or two.) To encourage dormancy, withhold water. When leaves yellow and fall off and stems separate from the tubers readily, lift the tubers, wash off the soil, and cure them in sun for several days or until

GLADIOLUS

GLADIOLUS

GLADIOLUS

GLADIOLUS TRISTIS

tubers are hard and dry. Be sure not to let portions of old stems adhere to the tubers; when they decay they also infect the tuber. Store the tubers in open flats in a cool, dry, frost-free place until time to start them into growth.

• Pests are not a serious menace to tuberous begonias. Slugs and snails can be controlled with poison baits. Control cyclamen mite with malathion. Brachyrinus weevil (also called black vine weevil or cyclamen borer) often attacks tubers. If you should happen to find evidence of weevils inside tubers, dig them out and treat the hole with sulfur and charcoal, then dust the whole tuber with diazinon.

Powdery mildew is the most common disease on tuberous begonias. It is a fungus that coats the leaves with a gray or white powdery dust and may spread over the entire plant. Spray or dust when the mildew first appears—or better still, spray as a preventive, starting when the plant has formed three leaves, and repeat every 10 days throughout the season. Controls are fungicides containing copper, lime sulfur, or sulfur; or a control that contains dinitro capryl phenyl crotonate.

Bletilla Striata

(Chinese ground orchid)
Tuberous root.
Hardy to semi-hardy.

Formerly called B. hyacinthina, it's one of the easiest of all terrestrial orchids to grow. Native to China and Japan, the plant produces three to six stiff, plaited pale green leaves and leafless 2-foot stalks carrying three to seven cattleya-shaped flowers 1½ inches long, of exquisite amethyst-purple. There is also a white form, B.s. alba. Bletillas start blooming in June and continue for about six weeks.

Use: Bletilla can be planted outdoors in light shade in all except the coldest sections of the country. It makes a charming pot plant to grow indoors or in lathhouses and other lightly shaded areas.

Culture: Plant "tubers" in the fall in a well drained high-humus soil such as you'd prepare for tuberous begonias. Provide ample moisture during the growing season. The plant becomes completely dormant in winter. In colder sections, mulch outdoor plantings with straw.

The plants eventually form large clumps which can be divided for increase, preferably in the early spring, just before growth starts. Bletilla can also be grown from seed.

Brodiaea

Corm. Hardy.

Some 25 or more species of brodiaea grow wild in many areas of the Western United States: in dry fields and moist meadows, along the coast, in valleys, in open woods, and on forested slopes. They bloom in spring or early summer, according to species.

Brodiaeas have a few grass-like leaves and slender stems topped with clusters of few to many tubular flowers, mostly in shades of blue, lilac, and white, and only occasionally in yellow, red, rose, or pink.

Listed here are four species available from specialists dealing in unusual or native plants—some as corms, others as seed. See *Ipheion uniflorum* for the species that was formerly called *B. uniflora*.

B. elegans (formerly called *B. coronaria*). Harvest brodiaea. When fields and hills begin to turn brown, this handsome brodiaea displays open clusters of 3 to 11 violet-purple flowers 1¼ to 1¾ inches long on 18-inch stems.

B. hyacinthina. White brodiaea. Open clusters of 10 to 40 bell-shaped, ½-inch-long white flowers, often tinged with purple and with greenish veins, bloom in June and July.

B. ida-maia. Firecracker flower. Each slender 1 to 3-foot-high stem bears an open cluster of 6 to 12 (or 23) pendulous, tubular scarlet flowers tipped with chrome green. They bloom from May to July.

B. laxa. Grass nut, Ithuriel's spear. Stout 1 to 2-foot-high stems bear open clusters of 8 to 48 violet-purple (rarely white), 1¼ to 1¾-inch-long flowers. It is very similar to harvest brodiaea but blooms earlier—April to June. It grows best in heavy soils.

Use: Most brodiaeas are ideal for naturalizing on hillsides and in out-of-the-way places that need not be watered in summer. Most of them do not perform well in areas with moist summers. But there are a few exceptions: *B. hyacinthina* often grows in low moist areas, and several species will take light shade under high branching deciduous trees.

Brodiaeas can also be planted in rock gardens. In cold climates, where they are not hardy, brodiaeas are grown in pots in the same way as freesias.

Culture: Best planted in sandy or gritty soils, although many will also grow in heavy soils if well-drained. They require lots of moisture during the growing season but should dry off completely in the summer. Plant corms 2 to 3 inches deep. In severe-winter climates, grow in pots in the same way as freesias; if planted in the ground, protect from freezing and thawing by covering with a thick mulch of leaves or straw.

DUTCH HYACINTHUS

HAEMANTHUS KATHERINAE

TALL BEARDED IRIS

HIPPEASTRUM

TALL BEARDED IRIS

Bulbinella

Tuberous root.
Tender.

Although there are a dozen species of bulbinella native to South Africa and New Zealand, the most popular and commonly available is *B. robusta* which forms a large clump of long, narrow, grass-like leaves. In January and February, clear, bright yellow flowers appear in spikes reminiscent of poker plant *(Kniphofia)*.

Use: In mild winter areas, this winter blooming plant makes a cheerful companion for viola, pansy, nemesia, snapdragon, and Iceland poppy. Bulbinella is splendid for cutting. In cold climates, grow it inside in containers.

Culture: Bulbinella is not fussy about soil, but requires good drainage. The plants perform best in half shade in inland areas. Provide ample moisture during the blooming season. After bloom, the plant becomes dormant; keep it dry during summer.

When signs of new growth appear in the early fall, start watering. Divide the clumps when they become very crowded. Bulbinella is easy to grow from seed sown in spring.

Calla lily, see *Zantedeschia.*

Caladium

Tuber. Tender.

The fancy-leafed caladiums, with their lush, arrow-shaped leaves, seem endlessly varied in their color patterns. Their interplay of red, pink, white, silver, and green makes them flamboyant companions for ferns, tuberous begonias, and fuchsias.

Use: In pots they become display plants; you can group them on a protected terrace, plunge them in the ground, or use them indoors as house plants.

These beautiful tropicals from South America are not temperamental. Except for the fact that they need slightly more heat, their cultural requirements are similar to those of tuberous begonias.

Culture: Good sized tubers produce satisfactory results; small bargain-priced tubers rarely perform well, especially in short summers in colder climates. Caladiums need four full months of growing time to store food in the tuber for next year's growth. If your area is slow to warm up in the spring, or if you want an early display, start the tubers indoors as early as March. You can start them in pots and move them outdoors when temperatures rise or start them in flats for transplanting into the ground when weather conditions permit. In flats, plant tubers 1 inch deep, using damp peat moss, leaf mold, or vermiculite. When white roots appear and top growth begins, they are ready for transplanting. In mild-winter climates, the middle of May is about the right time to start caladiums from tubers outdoors. Growth begins when daytime temperatures average 70°; tubers invariably rot if temperatures are lower.

A potting mixture of equal parts of coarse sand, loam, and peat moss or ground bark provides a loose, fibrous, well aerated soil that retains moisture well. Use a 5-inch pot for each 2½-inch tuber or a 7-inch pot for one larger or two smaller tubers. Place broken pot fragments at the bottom to improve the drainage. Fill pot half full of soil mix, stir in a teaspoon of complete commercial fertilizer, and mix it well with the soil. Add 1 inch of soil mix. Set the tuber with the knobby side up and cover with 2 inches of mix, bringing the soil within an inch of the rim. Water thoroughly.

Individual leaves last about three weeks. When a leaf is past its prime, pull it down and break or cut it off even with the rim of the pot. The stub dries rapidly and soon sloughs off.

In fall, gradually withhold water until all of leaves die down. Then lift the tubers from the soil and carefully remove most of the clinging soil. Tubers left in the ground after foliage dies may rot. Lay the tubers in a flat and let them dry for about 10 days in a semi-shaded location. Dust them thoroughly with a preparation containing both an insecticide and a fungicide. Store the tubers in dry peat moss or vermiculite with temperature above 50°.

Infrequent attacks by aphids and red spider mites are controlled with malathion. Spread bait for snails and slugs which like the young leaves.

Calochortus

(Mariposa lily, globe tulip)
Corm. Semi-hardy.

Delightful Western natives with slender stems and showy cup-shaped or globe-shaped flowers in white, yellow, bluish or lilac shades.

C. albus. Fairy lantern. Slender stems to 2 feet bear white 1¼-inch flowers resembling dainty, nodding lanterns. Blooms March to May. Needs protection in Northeast.

C. amabilis. Golden fairy lantern. Similar to *C. albus* but lower growing to 15 inches, with deep yellow, lantern-like flowers, often tinged with brown. Must be protected in Northeast.

C. amoenus. Purple globe tulip. Rosy-purple lanterns carried on 1½-foot stems. Variety 'Major' is a robust form to 24 inches with many branched stems.

C. coeruleus. Cat's ear. Exquisite, bluish, 1-inch-wide, open, cup-like flowers, furry inside. Grows 3 to 6 inches high. Blooms in March and April.

C. venustus. Mariposa tulip, butterfly tulip. Erect branched stems to 10 inches or more hold showy cup-shaped flowers in white or pale lilac, with reddish-brown markings. Blooms in May and June.

Use: The very names—fairy lanterns and cat's ears—suggest the charm and whimsical character of these plants. They adapt beautifully to rock garden and woodsy situations. Mariposa tulips naturalize on open sunny slopes and in rock gardens.

Culture: Plant corms 2 to 3 inches deep in September to December in the West. Calochortus is not hardy in the Midwest or Northeast except in sheltered locations near buildings; it also suffers from moist summers in these colder climates. In western Oregon and Washington, calochortus must be dug each year and stored in dry soil or sand until planting time, or the ground must be kept dry with a plastic sheet during the dormant period. These corms will not stand moisture while resting.

Globe tulips and cat's ear, both woodland plants, require light shade, loose soil, leaf mold, and plenty of water during the growing season. Mariposa tulip, growing natively in open fields, blooms in the sun. It can take heavier soil but must have good drainage and must be kept dry in summer. If you want to try growing calochortus in colder areas, apply a thick mulch in late fall to prevent alternate freezing and thawing; remove the mulch in early spring. Calochortus can also be potted and grown indoors.

Camassia

Bulb. Hardy.

Camass, or camassias, are among the loveliest of spring blooming wildlings. Most of them are native to moist meadows

and valleys in the West. Their white, cream, blue, or purple flowers bloom profusely in early spring from a basal cluster of long narrow leaves.

C. cusickii. This native of Oregon produces dense clusters of pale blue flowers on stems 3 to 4 feet tall; numerous basal leaves are 1 inch wide.

C. quamash. A species found growing wild along the coast and inland from California to British Columbia, partial to open, wet meadows. The finest forms are beautiful garden flowers with loose clusters of ultramarine blue flowers on 2½ to 3-foot stems.

C. leichtlinii. This is the handsomest of the camassias, growing to 4 feet. It bears large clusters of starry, blue-violet, rarely white to cream blooms in March in its native West, in May to early June in the East. The flowers open successively from the bottom to the top of the stalk; as flower segments fade, they twist interestingly.

Use: Although camassias are typically plants of meadow, marsh, and field, they are effective in borders, where their distinctive flowers add grace and color in early spring. They are ideal for naturalizing in moist places; clumps can remain undisturbed for many years.

Culture: Plant the bulbs 4 inches deep and 4 to 6 inches apart in a fairly heavy soil. The recommended planting time is fall, but if the weather remains warm, wait until later (about November) so that the bulbs will not be encouraged to root prematurely. Provide ample water during the growing season. Leaves dry up quickly after bloom.

Canna

Tuberous root.
Semi-hardy.

These tropical looking plants with brilliant, lily-like flowers add an exotic touch to your garden. Cannas are tender in colder climates where they should be stored indoors.

Flowers of cannas come in an extensive range of colors: white through ivory to shades of yellow and orange; pale to deep pink, apricot, coral, and salmon; and in many shades of red. There are also bicolors with blotches, stripes, or marginal markings.

The large, broad leaves are clear, bright green, blue-green, or a rich, polished bronze.

There are three main types of cannas. Lower growing and dwarf varieties include the French or Crozy cannas, from 3 to 4 feet tall, with large flower trusses; the Pfitzer Dwarf cannas from Germany, which grow 2½ to 3 feet tall; and the Seven Dwarfs series. These latter plants, only 18 inches high, are easily started from seed, reach flowering size within about 12 weeks, and bloom throughout the summer.

The Italian, or orchid-flowered cannas, are tall (4 to 5½ feet), and the flower segments are more open and spreading than the French cannas.

The third group includes all the other cannas, most of which are the tall (5 to 6 feet), old-fashioned cannas with smaller flowers and less foliage.

Use: Cannas are usually at their best in groups of a single color seen against a plain background such as a fence or evergreen shrubs. Small groups of low growing cannas are effective with large rocks, by stone steps, or grouped in front of a rock wall. They make striking poolside plantings if placed so that their bold form and bright color are reflected.

You can grow cannas in large tubs or pots on a terrace or patio or in a sunny corner of a lanai. Leaves are useful in arrangements, but cut flowers don't last.

Culture: Start seed over bottom heat in early spring; plants should be ready to go outside in May in milder sections, in June in colder areas. Nick the tough-coated seeds with a file or knife or soak in water overnight to speed up germination. Since cannas from seed will be in mixed colors and sizes, put plants in an out-of-the-way bed until you can sort them for garden use.

You can also buy rootstocks of named varieties. Start in flats or pots in early spring in subdued light with bottom heat. Keep them in a warm place until they sprout, then bring them into the light and keep warm. When the ground warms up, set them out.

Wait until May or June to plant canna rootstocks in the garden. If you start the plants inside in March, they may bloom by August. (The blooming season lasts until late fall in warmer sections.) If you start them outside, bloom will be two weeks later.

Cannas do best in rich, loose soil with as much sunlight and heat as they can get. Planted in containers, tuberous rootstocks can be placed close together. For massed garden planting, set them about 5 inches deep and 10 inches apart. Normal spacing is about 18 inches. Give them plenty of water during the growing season. Pick off the faded blossoms to prevent energy from going into seed production. After all the flowers in the cluster have bloomed, cut off the stalk as close to the ground as possible.

In milder climates, cannas may be left in the ground throughout the year. In the fall, simply cut back faded flower stalks and leaves to make room for new growth. Divide crowded clumps and replant separate rootstocks in spring. Here is how to handle cannas in colder areas: after the first frost in the fall, cut off the stalks and leaves and dig up the rootstocks; let them dry.

Dust the cut ends with a disinfectant and store them stem side down in a box of dry sand, peat moss, vermiculite, or kiln-dried sawdust. Canna rootstocks keep best in a cool dry place under root-cellar conditions. In the spring, cut the rootstocks into 2 or 3-inch pieces, dust again, and plant.

Chionodoxa

(Glory-of-the-snow)
Bulb. Hardy.

These appealing and beautiful little bulbs from Asia Minor are extremely hardy and perform best where winters are cold. They have received their common name from their habit of coming into flower through the melting snow in mountain meadows.

C. luciliae is most frequently grown and generally available. It produces strap-shaped leaves and 6-inch stems with as many as 10 brilliant blue, white centered, star-like flowers that open soon after the stalk emerges above the ground. A horticultural variety, 'Alba,' has somewhat larger white flowers.

C. sardensis is a favorite with many because of its deep, true gentian-blue flowers accented by a very small white eye.

Use: Lovely in intimate, partially shaded spots; in rock gardens; under early flowering deciduous shrubs. Chionodoxas make a wonderful carpet under forsythia, which blooms at the same time.

Culture: Plant bulbs 3 inches deep in September or October in half shade in soil with lots of humus; give plenty of moisture while growing; in western Oregon and Washington bulbs can be planted in full sun. Divide clumps when they become crowded— or about every three or four years. Under favorable conditions, chionodoxas seed themselves and create beautiful drifts of color year after year.

Clivia Miniata

(Kaffir lily)
Tuberous root. Tender.

A member of the amaryllis family, clivia was first discovered in Natal, South Africa. In March and April brilliant clusters of orange, funnel-shaped blooms rise from dense clumps of dark green strap-shaped leaves.

Plantsmen have been hybridizing clivias to obtain sturdier, more floriferous plants with a wider range of colors. As a result, today we have a wide selection of hybrid clivias which include the Belgian hybrids (deep red-orange blooms on thick rigid stalks held above clumps of very wide, dark green leaves) and the Zimmerman hybrids (flowers in white and soft shades of yellow, orange, or red), ranging 1½ to 2 feet in height. Red berries follow the flowers.

Use: In warm frostless areas, clivias are striking in shady borders with such companion plants as ferns, cinerarias, and azaleas. They also make excellent container plants, since they thrive when their roots are crowded. In cold climates grow clivias in pots indoors or on protected terraces. The plants can be stored in a light cellar over the winter.

Culture: Clivias need ample light (not direct sun) and good air circulation (but not drafts) for best growth. Unlike most other bulbs, clivias should not be dried off after flowering. Keep the roots moist at all times. In November, when growth slows down, water less frequently but never let the foliage wilt.

Plant clivia with the top of the root mass just above the soil line. Use rich, fairly heavy soil that is well drained. Fertilize the plants two or three times during the growing season with a water-soluble commercial fertilizer. Clivias should not be disturbed frequently; plan to leave them in one place for several years. Increase numbers by division of well-established plants.

Colchicum Autumnale

(Autumn crocus, meadow saffron)
Corm. Hardy.

Planted or unplanted, with or without soil, the shiny brown corms of this plant faithfully send up their blooms in August or September. Despite one of its common names, this colchicum is not a true crocus. It is a member of the lily family, whereas crocus belongs in the iris family.

The flowers of colchicum are light lavender-pink, white, or purple, larger than those of spring blooming crocus. Foliage is absent during the blooming period; it appears in spring in the form of broad, 12-inch leaves that yellow and dry rapidly in late May or early June, then disappear completely. This is the last you see of the plants until they again send up stemless, slender, long tubed flowers in fall.

Use: In the garden, colchicums provide an element of surprise on hot September days. They are useful and effective planted in groups along driveways or in out-of-the-way spots.

Perhaps their most common use is in pots or bowls. Since colchicums multiply rapidly, a few dozen corms will fill considerable space if you dig and reset them every two or three years.

Culture: Colchicums' dormant period is brief—from about July 1 to mid-August—so this is the time to make new plantings and reset crowded plantings. Plant the corms with the tips 3 or 4 inches deep. Provide a moist, well-drained loam.

Gardeners who find it difficult to combine the large leaves of colchicum with other plants can try planting corms in wire baskets. Sink the baskets where you want the plants to bloom, lift them when flowers fade, and plant the corms in a less conspicuous place to finish their growth cycle. Plant pests and diseases, as well as rodents, seem to ignore colchicums. If you plant corms in pots, set them with tips 2 inches under the soil mixture.

When planting colchicums in bowls, place the corms securely and upright on 1 or 2 inches of pebbles or set them in a 2 or 3-inch layer of fiber, filling the containers with water until it touches the base of the corms. Replenish water as needed to keep it to the proper level.

Crinum

(Veld lily)
Bulb. Semi-hardy.

Crinums, natives of tropical and subtropical regions, are interesting and often spectacular members of the amaryllis family. They have handsome, broad, thick, strap-shaped leaves, mostly evergreen; in spring or summer they produce clusters of fragrant, showy, white, whitish, or pink trumpet-shaped flowers, often striped or tinged with red. Individual blooms are sometimes 6 inches long.

C. asiaticum. This plant forms large clumps of upright, tropical looking, 3-foot-long leaves. Its stalks bear 20 or more pure white, extremely fragrant flowers that bloom continuously over a long period. Mature bulbs may weigh as much as 50 pounds.

C. bulbispermum, formerly called *C. longifolium,* once the most commonly grown of the crinums, can be grown in milder areas; it is not hardy in the Southeast. Its bright pink flowers, deeper red on the outside, bloom long and profusely.

C. mooreii is characterized by long, thin, strap-shaped, prominently veined, wavy margined, bright green leaves. The bell-shaped flowers are rosy pink or pinkish red and very fragrant.

C. powellii, a hybrid between *C. bulbispermum* and *C. mooreii,* has dark rose-colored flowers; 'Alba,' a pure white form, is said to be as beautiful as the Easter lily.

Use: Where winters are mild, crinums may be grown in half shaded borders where, after the large bulbs are well established, they make impressively large clumps. They are effective combined with agapanthus, whose blue flowers bloom at the same time.

In sections too cold to grow crinums outside, plant the bulbs in large pots, tubs, or boxes; move into a protected area during the winter months.

Culture: Plant in partial shade in soil that has been thoroughly prepared with leaf mold, peat moss, or other humus. Although bulbs are available throughout the year from a few sources, fall and spring are preferred planting times. Set the bulb about 6 inches under the surface of the ground. It may take a year for some species to become established. Water generously during spring and summer. Bulbs can be transplanted during the dormant season, but it is best not to disturb them oftener than necessary.

Crocus

Corm. Hardy.

In climates where they grow best, you can enjoy crocus in bloom in your garden for at least seven months of the year. These hardy, fascinating members of the iris family, native to the Mediterranean region and Southwest Asia, include autumn flowering species that bloom from late August to late November; winter flowering species that give color from December to mid-February; and spring-flowering species that carry on from mid-February to March. Added to this bounty are the large flowered Dutch crocus, derived from *C. vernus;* these start blooming in late January or early February and continue into March. (In the Midwest and Northeast, most blooming times mentioned for winter and spring blooming species and the large Dutch crocus will be at least a month later.)

Crocus have basal, grass-like leaves, sometimes with a silvery midrib, appearing before, with, or after the flowers. The slender tubular flowers, flaring at the top, are practically stemless—the extremely short stem is hidden underground. What looks like a stem above ground actually is the tube of the flower.

Nurseries generally stock several varieties of large Dutch crocus and a small number of species; however, dealers specializing in unusual bulbs can supply quite a selection of species and varieties.

Species Crocus

Though species crocus usually have smaller blooms, they often produce many more flowers to a corm than the large Dutch crocus. Following are a few of the best known species:

C. speciosus. This is the best known and also the showiest of the autumn-flowering species. It has large blue-violet flowers with 4-inch tubes, and brilliant vermilion-orange stigmas. Named varieties are available in pale and dark blue, lavender, and white flowers whose segments measure up to 3 inches in length. This species increases rapidly by seed and division. Corms often bloom within a few days after being planted; unplanted corms sometimes also bloom.

C. kotschyanus (formerly called *C. zonatus*). This September blooming species has delicate pinkish lavender or lilac flowers with white stamens.

C. ancyrensis, orange-yellow, the earliest spring crocus.

C. chrysanthus, one of the most beautiful, has sweet scented, orange-yellow flowers with black tipped anthers.

C. sieberi, delicate lavender-blue flowers with a golden throat. One of the most beautiful species. In the Northeast it blooms as soon as the snow melts in early March.

C. susianus, the cloth of gold crocus, has brilliant orange-gold, star-like flowers, each segment having a dark brown stripe down the center. It blooms in January or February in the West, March in the Midwest and East.

C. tomasinianus is one of the most engaging and easily grown species, having slender buds and star-shaped flowers of silvery lavender-blue, sometimes with a dark blotch on the tip of each segment. It is extremely prolific when well established, covering the ground with its bloom in late January or early February in more moderate climates, March in colder areas.

Dutch Crocus

These garden forms developed by the Dutch from the species *C. vernus* start blooming with the last of the later blooming species and continue into March (April in coldest areas). Vigorous and adapted to a wider range of climates than the species crocus, they are the only crocus planted to any extent in mild-winter areas, such as Southern California.

Dutch crocus are listed in catalogs and sold in nurseries by color: white, yellow, blue, or purple and feathered white and purple.

Use: Plant at the base of early spring flowering shrubs or flowering trees. For a delightful spring surprise, tuck some crocus corms in spaces between bricks or paving stones. Rock gardens, raised beds, and dry rock walls also suit them well.

Crocus naturalize easily in lawns and can be planted for an effective combination under any ground cover that will let the tops push through. Such a cover will help to keep mud from splattering the crocus flowers; but you have to control companion plants so they don't crowd the crocus.

Culture: Plant corms as soon as available in the fall. Set them 2 or 3 inches deep, in light, sandy soil (they will grow in almost any soil if it's well drained). Although crocus perform best in full sun, they will grow in filtered shade. They increase quite rapidly and should be divided every three or four years. In some areas, field mice eat the corms; chipmunks also consider them a delicacy and carry them away to replant in other places. A group of 25 corms is colorful, but 100 or more make a real show. If you plant them in lawns, don't mow off foliage before it ripens.

Cyclamen

Tuber. Hardy, semi-hardy, and tender.

Several species of cyclamen, members of the primrose family, are available in nurseries. The best known, of course, is the showy florists' cyclamen, a popular potted plant during the winter months, especially around Christmas time. Not so well known but especially worthwhile, particularly in cold climates, are the engaging, smaller flowered, hardy cyclamen. A special bonus is their decorative heart-shaped leaves, often marbled with silver or white. And in milder climates, there's hardly a month in the year when some hardy cyclamen isn't in bloom. Both the florists' and hardy forms have flowers with reflexed petals that remind you of shooting stars.

In the following list, all but one, *C. persicum,* the florists' cyclamen, are called hardy cyclamen.

C. europaeum. Distinctly fragrant crimson flowers on 5 to 6-inch stems. Bright green foliage is mottled silver white. It appears before the flowers and is almost evergreen. This is one of the most reliable species for colder climates. It blooms from July to November in the Northwest and in northern California; in September and October in the Northeast. Quite partial to shade.

C. persicum. Florists' cyclamen. Tender to half-hardy. Many strains are available, with exceptionally large flowers in white or shades of pink or rose on 6 to 8-inch stems. It blooms from November to April. There are kinds with double, crested, or fringed flowers. Leaves are green or varigated.

C. neapolitanum. Many rose-pink flowers bloom on 4 to 6-inch stems. Variety 'Album' has dainty white blooms. Large, light green, extremely handsome leaves marbled silver and white with smooth to wavy edges appear after the flowers. This is the most vigorous and easily grown species and one of the most reliable for colder climates. It blooms from late August to mid-October.

Use: Hardy cyclamen make delightful carpets under camellias and rhododendrons. They are also effective in shaded sections in a rock garden. An attractive planting: a small plateau in a rock garden with *C. neapolitanum* and woodsy moss under maidenhair ferns. For portable color they can be grown for a season or two in pots and plunged into the ground where you need them, but in the long run they do best in the ground.

If you live in a mild winter section, you can grow the larger flowered florists' cyclamen outdoors in the same kinds of situations in which you would plant tuberous begonias for summer color. In fact, many gardeners rotate these two plants for color in the shade throughout most of the year.

Culture: Hardy cyclamen do best in moderately rich, well drained soil with ample humus. If your soil is poor, work in balanced fertilizer mixed with compost before planting. Add a light annual topdressing of the same material if plants show signs of weakness. No other fertilizer is needed.

Plant tubers about 6 to 10 inches apart and cover with 1 inch of soil. *C. neapolitanum* increases in size more rapidly than others, so plant its corms about 12 inches apart.

You can plant or transplant cyclamen almost any time of year, but the ideal time is the brief dormant period during June, July, or August. If transplanting during the growing season, be careful not to let the leaves or roots dry out.

Gently work a light mulch of leaf mold, peat moss, or similar material into the soil to help hold moisture and reduce weeds. Don't cultivate near tubers; they are shallow rooted and can be easily damaged.

Although hardy cyclamen stand dry periods with no apparent injury you will get maximum tuber development if you keep the soil moist.

Florists' cyclamen have similar cultural requirements, except that they grow best in a slightly acid soil. The tubers should be planted so that the upper half protrudes above the level of the soil. If they are planted too deep, water may settle in the crown and cause rot.

Propagation of cyclamen is best from seed, for division is slow and uncertain. Because the seed pods mature in mid summer and crack open easily to the touch, collect the sticky seed and dry at room temperature for several days. Sow this seed in late summer or early fall under glass where night temperatures can be maintained at 60°F. Germination will occur in three to six weeks. Shade the seedlings until shorter days arrive. If you sow in mid-August, you can transplant in December (100 plants to a standard 14 by 20-inch flat).

If you prefer—and can wait a year longer for blooms—sow seed outdoors in a well prepared bed in early fall in mild climates or in spring if conditions are severe. The seedlings can be transplanted the second summer.

Dahlia

Tuber. Tender.

Dahlia flowers are divided into eight size groups, ranging from a generous 8 inches or more in diameter to the smallest pompon not more than 2 inches in diameter. To help you become familiar with the diverse forms these profusely blooming summer bulbs take, here is a classification list of various flower forms of dahlias:

SINGLE. Blooms have a single row of florets.

MIGNON. Single flowers that grow on plants about 18 inches high.

ORCHID-FLOWERED. Like single dahlias except that the rays (petals) are involute for at least two-thirds of their length.

ANEMONE. Blooms have one or more rows of ray florets (incomplete florets—with a pistil but no stamens) surrounding a dense group of tubular florets.

COLLARETTE. Blooms have a single outer row of flat ray florets and one or more internal rows of small florets surrounding the disc (center of flower head).

PEONY. Blooms have two or more rows of ray florets surrounding a disc.

INCURVED CACTUS. Fully double blooms show no disc. The margins of the majority of the ray florets are fully revolute for at least one half of their length. The pointed rays curve toward center of bloom.

STRAIGHT CACTUS. Fully double blooms show no disc. The majority of the ray florets are fully revolute for at least half their length. The pointed rays are straight, slightly incurved, or recurved.

SEMI-CACTUS. Fully double blooms have pointed ray florets that are revolute for less than half their length, broad at base and straight or incurving.

FORMAL DECORATIVE. Fully double blooms show no disc. The rays are broad and either pointed or rounded at their tips. Most are in a regular arrangement. The margins of the outer floral rays are flat or slightly revolute and tend to recurve; the central rays are cupped.

INFORMAL DECORATIVE. Fully double blooms show no disc. The margins of most of the floral rays are slightly or not at all revolute. The rays are long, twisted or pointed and usually irregular in arrangement.

BALL. Fully double blooms are ball shaped or slightly flattened at the top. The ray florets have blunt or rounded tips and are cupped for more than half their length.

POMPON. Blooms are similar to those of ball dahlias but more globular and of miniature size, with florets involute for their whole length.

Use: As cut flowers, dahlias are valued for their varied forms and sizes and for an extensive range of colors and hues that lack only true blue. Lower growing, bushy kinds make gay, easy-going bedding plants. If grouped in masses of one color, rather than in mixed colors, the taller dahlias look handsome among and in front of shrubs in wide borders, along driveways, and against high walls or fences.

Culture: Despite their Mexican ancestry—which suggests that they are hot-climate plants—dahlias grow best in coastal areas where summers are cool.

If you live near the coast, plant dahlias in full sun; in very hot areas, provide a spot where they will receive light shade during the hottest part of the day. Wait until the weather warms up. When the time is right for corn, potatoes, and tomatoes, it's right for dahlias, too.

Dig the soil at least 1 foot deep. In sandy soil, incorporate humus (leaf mold, peat moss, compost); lighten heavy soils with organic materials and sand.

If you use fertilizer at planting time, thoroughly incorporate $\frac{1}{4}$ cup of complete fertilizer into the soil in the bottom of a 10-inch deep hole, then place 4 inches of plain, well pulverized soil on top of it. If you use manure, leach out excess salts by an extra heavy watering. Set a stake in the hole and place the tuber in a horizontal position with the eye pointing in the direction of the stake and 2 inches away from it. Cover the tuber with 3 inches of soil. In warm areas, water thoroughly after planting; in sections of the country where late spring rains are frequent, it is seldom necessary to water at planting time. As the shoots grow, gradually fill the basin with soil. To grow dahlias without staking: place two tubers 4 to 6 inches apart in a wider hole with eyes facing one another; as the plants grow they will support each other.

Water after planting and not again until shoots appear above the ground—unless, of course, there is a long hot dry spell. As plants grow and develop large leaf surfaces, increase watering.

Apply a mulch around the plants to keep down weeds, prevent evaporation, and cool the soil in warm climates. Mulches also reduce the need for cultivating which might damage surface roots.

When the plant has formed three sets of leaves, pinch out the center stalk to force side branching and produce a bushy and profusely flowered plant. If you want large flowers, remove all except the terminal buds on the side stalks. For a second bloom, pinch back the side stalks one joint from the main stem. New flower-producing lateral shoots will develop below the cut. Pinch smaller flowering varieties, such as pompons, only once; from then on, keep the flowers picked regularly.

After the tops of dahlias turn yellow or have been frosted, cut stalks to within 6 inches of the ground. Dig a circle around the plant, 1 foot from the center, and gently pry up the clump with a spading fork, shaking off loose soil. In handling, be careful not to damage the brittle tubers. Let the clumps dry in the sun for several hours.

From here on, experts differ as to procedure. Some favor dividing the clumps immediately to save storage space. Freshly dug tubers are easy to cut; it is also easier to recognize the buds at this time. Many experts, though, advise leaving clumps intact, since there is less danger of shriveling when stored in cellars. They divide the clumps in spring when the eyes start to grow.

To store whole clumps, cover with dry sand, sawdust, peat moss, perlite, or vermiculite; store in a cool (40° to 45°) dry place. About two to four weeks before planting in the spring, separate tubers by cutting from the stalk with a sharp knife; leave 1 inch of stalk attached to each tuber, which must have an eye or bud in order to produce a new plant. Place tubers in moist sand to encourage development of sprouts.

If clumps are divided immediately after digging in fall, dust the cut surfaces with sulfur to prevent rot, bury the tubers in sand, sawdust, or vermiculite, and store in a cool dry place.

Daffodil, see *Narcissus.*

Dierama

(Fairy wand, wand flower)
Corm. Semi-hardy.

Beautiful and unique, this South African plant is closely related to ixia and sparaxis. It has evergreen, narrow, sword-like leaves; unbelievably slender stems, 4 to 6 or sometimes 7 feet, arch gracefully under the weight of the bright purple, pink, or white, pendulous, bell-shaped flowers on the upper half of the stems. They bloom in late summer and fall.

D. pendula. Flowers are white or bluish white to pale or dark mauve, up to 1 inch long in slender drooping spikes.

D. pulcherrima. Similar in growth habit to the foregoing but larger and more vigorous, with larger flowers to 1½ inches long in bright purple or almost red. There is also a white variety. Leaves are extremely rigid and are broader and longer than those of *D. pendula.*

Use: Plant dieramas where the delicate stems and pendant blossoms stand out clearly—as on the edge of a pool or stream, on an upslope, or on the border of a lawn. They make interesting container plants.

Culture: Set the large corms 3 inches deep and 6 inches apart in fall. Provide a sunny location in deep, rich, moist soil and give the plants lots of water during the growing season.

In the East, dierama is hardy as far north as Washington, D.C. In colder areas, put five or six corms in a 10-inch pot and grow in a cool greenhouse.

Eranthis Hyemalis

(Winter aconite)
Tuber. Hardy.

A rewarding sight in cold climates is the appearance of the pixie-like winter aconite soon after the first snowdrops start to bloom. Each charming, yellow, buttercup-like flower, 1 to 1½ inches across, tops a 3 to 8-inch stem above a frilly collar of bright green leafy bracts. Basal leaves, like the bracts, are divided into many narrow segments.

Use: Naturalize in woodland-type settings, planting in colonies among snowdrops, *Scilla sibirica,* and early crocus. It is effective in shallow pots or boxes.

Culture: Plant as early as possible in fall. Set tubers 3 inches deep and 3 to 4 inches apart in spongy, porous soil in part shade. Provide lots of moisture while plant is growing and in bloom. It is best to divide sections of clumps rather than to separate and replant single tubers. The species increases by self-sown seed.

TALL BEARDED IRIS   DUTCH IRIS

TALL BEARDED IRIS   45

Erythronium

(Dog-tooth violet, fawn lily)
Corm. Hardy.

Gardeners who know the purple or rose-flowered European-Asian species *E. dens-canis,* with its handsome mottled leaves, may call all erythroniums dog-tooth violets, but this name rightly applies only to this species. The name fawn lily comes from the fact that several species have their leaves mottled with bronze or brown.

Two other common names of the fawn lily indicate their time of bloom. In the central Rocky Mountains, they're sometimes known as Easter bells because they bloom about Easter time. Elsewhere, they are called trout lilies, since their flowering coincides with the opening of trout season.

E. americanum. Common adder's tongue, trout lily. This familiar North American native grows from Canada to Florida and west to Arkansas. Leaves are mottled purplish brown and whitish; solitary yellow flowers are sometimes tinged with pink. It grows 1 foot high. Under ideal conditions, corms multiply rapidly to form colonies.

E. californicum. California fawn lily. Leaves are heavily mottled with brown; creamy white or yellow flowers have a transverse band of darker color. The variety 'Bicolor' has white, yellow-centered flowers that look up at you; they are beautifully fragrant.

E. hendersonii. Southern Oregon is the native habitat of this species with mottled leaves and light to dark lavender flowers with deep maroon centers. It grows to 12 inches.

E. oregonum, formerly *E. giganteum.* A native of the Cascade Mountains from Washington to northern California, this plant has mottled leaves and large creamy flowers with a yellow base on stems 8 to 12 inches high.

E. revolutum. This Western species is similar to *E. californicum,* having lightly mottled leaves and large rose-pink or lavender flowers, banded yellow at the base, on erect 1-foot stems.

E. tuolumnense. Found in the open woodland in California's Sierra Nevada foothills, this species has all-green leaves and deep yellow flowers, greenish yellow at the base. Stems are 12 to 15 inches high. This is the most robust of all erythroniums.

Use: They're such dainty lilies that, planted singly, they go practically unnoticed. But scattered informally under trees, by a pool, along a shady path, or in rock gardens, their graceful nodding flowers in late April and May compel your attention.

Culture: Plant corms in the fall in shade or part shade. Set them 2 to 3 inches deep, 4 to 5 inches apart, in well-drained woodland soil. Unlike other bulbs, they need water during the summer months; a peat moss mulch helps to retain moisture. Divide corms in fall only when they get crowded.

Eucomis

(Pineapple flower)
Bulb. Hardy.

These natives of South Africa look surprisingly similar to pineapples. In mid summer thick, 2 to 3-foot-tall spikes of ½-inch-long flowers are topped by tufts of leaf-like bracts. The scented, greenish white flowers are sometimes tinged pink or purple. The 2-foot-long strap-shaped leaves are deeply creased with wavy margins.

Use: These handsome plants are good garden or container subjects.

Culture: Pineapple flower needs a sunny, well-drained site. In the garden, plant bulbs 6 inches deep in rich soil with plenty of humus; set bulbs about a foot apart to avoid crowding the foliage. Plant bulbs in the ground as soon as possible in the fall. Be sure to water during the summer. To grow in pots, plant bulbs just below the soil surface in spring. Garden-grown bulbs can be left for several years before dividing, but container grown ones should have their soil replenished each year. To propagate eucomis, remove offset bulbs from the parent bulb when it is lifted or repotted in the fall. (You can also grow them from seed, but it takes about five years to obtain flowers.)

Freesia Refracta

Corm. Tender.

Ambrosial fragrance and excellence as cut flowers endear freesias to those who grow them. In spring, slender, wiry branched stems with a few leaves are topped with one-sided spikes of 2-inch-long, greenish yellow to bright yellow tubular flowers. Plants grow up to 18 inches and have basal grass-like leaves. Crosses between *F. refracta* and *F. armstrongii* (white tube

'BLACK DRAGON' LILY

'CRIMSON BEAUTY' LILY

'ENCHANTMENT' LILY

'GOLDEN SPLENDOR' LILY

IXIA

47

orange at base, segments edged with rose-purple) have resulted in hybrids with large flowers in a range of colors that includes purple, orange, pink.

Use: In milder climates, the best way to grow freesias is to plant them in beds where you can enjoy their fragrance, pick them for bouquets, and conveniently forget them while they go through the necessary post-bloom, drying-off period. Grow them in containers for close-up pleasure; in the East, Midwest, and Northwest, plant freesias in pots and let them bloom in a sunny window while snow lies on the ground outside. To develop finer flowers on freesias grown inside, maintain cooler temperatures at night (down to 40°).

Culture: Plant in full sun in light, well-drained soil. Set the corms 2 inches deep with the pointed end up, spacing them 2 inches apart; when planted close together, the floppy plants hold each other up. Support freesias growing in pots by placing small bamboo stakes around the perimeter, and encircling the stakes with several tiers of raffia, coarse thread, twine, or plastic ribbon used for tying plants.

Fritillaria

(Fritillary)
Bulb. Hardy.

The fritillarias, members of the lily family, are unusual and little known as garden plants probably because most of them do not adapt outside their native woodland habitat. Fortunately, the fritillarias which are easiest to grow also happen to be the showiest of the genus. They are the first two species listed below:

F. imperialis. Crown imperial. The giant among fritillarias, this is a regal looking plant with a stout, 3½ to 4-foot purple-spotted stalk clothed from the ground up with broad, glossy leaves. In mid spring it is topped with a cluster of pendant red, orange, or yellow bells crowned with a tuft of leaves. On the debit side, the plant has an unpleasant odor.

F. meleagris. Checkered lily, Snakeshead. Although modest looking in comparison to the crown imperial, this fritillaria is nevertheless quite showy with its nodding, 2-inch bells, large for the size of the plant, on slender 12 to 18-inch stems. The flowers, checkered and veined with reddish brown and purple on a paler background, bloom in late spring. A pure white variety is handsome when contrasted with the darker ones. This species is native to England, Europe, and Southwest Asia. It is remarkably permanent in colder climates.

F. pudica. Yellow fritillary. This native of northern California north to British Columbia, east to Montana and Wyoming, has one to three soft yellow or orange bells (April to June) that turn brick red with age. Stems are 6 to 12 inches high with three to eight long narrow leaves.

F. recurva. Scarlet fritillary. You'll find this the brightest of the native Western fritillarias. From March to July, scarlet bells flecked with yellow inside, tinged purple outside, bloom on leafy stems up to 2½ feet high. It grows well in southern Oregon, northern California, and western Nevada.

F. lanceolata. Checker lily. In coastal mountains of California, north to British Columbia, and east to Idaho, the checker lily blooms from February to May. Its nodding, bowl-shaped bells are brownish purple, mottled with yellow or pale greenish yellow and lightly stippled with purple. Stems grow to 2½ feet high and have whorls of 4 to 6-inch-long leaves.

Use: The crown imperial, like other lilies, is effective in borders against a quiet green background of shrubs or among non-invasive plants in perennial borders. It can also be grown in large pots. The smaller fritillarias adapt to woodland settings and are excellent in rock gardens.

Culture: Plant fritillarias as soon as available in early fall in a well-drained, porous soil containing ample humus. Provide full sun for the crown imperial in coastal areas, filtered shade where summers are hot. The small kinds definitely require filtered shade. Set bulbs of the crown imperial 4 to 5 inches deep; plant bulbs of the smaller species 3 to 4 inches under the soil surface.

Galanthus

(Snowdrop)
Bulb. Hardy.

In cold climates where they grow best, brave little snowdrops are often the first bulbs to bloom. There are more than a dozen species native mostly to the eastern Mediterranean region, but the two listed below are generally offered by bulb dealers. Snowdrops are often confused with snowflakes (*Leucojum*) to which they are closely related. Both have white, bell-shaped flowers with green tipped segments, but the snowdrop has green tips on inner flower segments only—the three outer (and larger) segments have no green tips. Another difference: the inner segments of the snowdrop's flower are smaller than the outer segments, whereas the snowflake's segments are all alike.

G. elwesii. Giant snowdrop. Waxy, white, globular, green-spotted bells, 1½ inches long, are borne singly on 12-inch stems above two or three basal, 8-inch-long leaves ¾ inch wide. In milder sections, it blooms as early as January in spells of mild weather—and invariably by February. In colder areas, flowers appear in March or even later.

G. nivalis. Common snowdrop. This charming small bulb has narrow (¼-inch) blue-green leaves and 6 to 9-inch stems topped with a single, nodding, 1-inch bell jauntily tipped with bright green on the inner segments.

Use: Snowdrops belong in woodland settings—in small pockets in rock gardens or in colonies under early spring flowering shrubs. They can also be grown in pots (plant eight bulbs to a 5-inch pot) for close-up winter pleasure. They naturalize beautifully in congenial surroundings.

Culture: Plant bulbs as soon as available in sun or half shade in a moist soil with a large proportion of humus. Set bulbs 3 to 4 inches deep and 2 to 3 inches apart. Plants can remain undisturbed for many years and be increased by seeds or offsets. Do not cut the leaves. The best time to move and divide snowdrop bulbs is when they are growing or just after flowering. Lift with soil around the bulbs so as not to disturb the roots and replant immediately; do not let them dry out. Bulbs planted when dry often take a season to become established.

Galtonia Candicans

(Summer hyacinth)
Bulb. Semi-hardy.

Another South African native, the summer hyacinth differs considerably from the common spring blooming hyacinth in appearance. It blooms in summer and early fall. Strap-like leaves are 2 to 3 feet long; stout 2 to 4-foot stems are topped with loose, spike-like clusters of drooping, funnel-shaped, 1 to 1½-inch long, fragrant, white flowers whose three outer segments are often tipped with green.

Use: Summer hyacinths add cool white and spiky form to summer borders. To hide the long floppy leaves, grow them behind lower, bushy plants. The bulbs can also be grown in containers.

Culture: In mild climates, plant the bulbs in autumn; wait until spring in colder areas. Set bulbs

about 6 inches deep in a well-drained soil in a sunny spot. Keep the soil moist throughout the active growing season. Spread bait for slugs that will otherwise consume the young growth. Bulbs may be left undisturbed in the ground for several years in areas where the ground doesn't freeze. In cold sections, bulbs are often hardy if mulched in winter. Some gardeners, however, dig the bulbs in the fall after the foliage dies down and dry and store bulbs at a temperature of 55° to 60°.

Gladiolus

Corm. Tender.

The name *Gladiolus* is derived from the Latin word *gladius*, which means sword, referring to the shape of the leaves. Flowers are funnel-shaped, usually flaring and ruffled, sometimes hooded, and almost always carried on a one-sided spike.

If you could gather all the gladiolus that are native to the Mediterranean area, tropical and South Africa, and the Mascarene Islands, your giant bouquet would include 200 to 250 different species. However, only a few of these members of the Iris family are available commercially in their wild forms. Most of the gladiolus we grow in our gardens are the result of hybridizing that has been going on for over 100 years. By far the most popular gladiolus are the glamorous, large flowered hybrids. Yet gardeners who appreciate dainty informal plants should not overlook the smaller flowered hybrids and a few species carried by specialists.

Large flowered gladiolus hybrids

Individual blooms may be as much as 8 inches across, and stems grow up to 4, 5, or even 6 feet. Hybrid gladiolus are divided into five series: the 100 (miniature) series has flowers less than 2 inches wide; the 200 (small) series, flowers 2 inches wide; the 300 (medium) series, flowers 3 inches wide; the 400 (large) series, flowers 4 inches wide; and the 500 (giant) series, flowers more than 5 inches wide. Flowers are usually self-colored but may have spots or flecks of other colors in the throat. The following color classification indicates the impressive range of color in the large flowered hybrid gladiolus: white or white and cream; light yellow and buff; orange; light salmon, deep salmon, scarlet; light red, deep red, or black red; light rose, deep rose, lavender, or lavender with shading; purple, light violet, deep violet; smoky shades; other shades.

(Continued on page 51)

MUSCARI   LARGE-CUPPED NARCISSUS

TAZETTA HYBRID NARCISSUS   NARCISSUS BULBOCODIUM

(Continued from page 49)
Species and small flowered hybrids

The following gladiolus are important to any gardener who wishes to explore beyond the large flowered kinds:

G. colvillei. This red-and-yellow flowered gladiolus is presumably the first garden hybrid gladiolus ever introduced and is the forerunner of a small flowered hybrid race called baby gladiolus. Baby gladiolus have a delightful informal charm; their open or flaring flowers, 2½ to 3¼ inches in diameter, appear loosely in short spikes on 18-inch stems.

Since the wild ancestors of baby gladiolus grow in the higher, wetter regions of the South African Cape, these hybrids are adapted to mild, damp, cool coastal areas where they bloom in May and June. In the Northwest, they flower in late June and early July; in the East, baby gladiolus can be grown only under glass north of Washington, D.C.

G. primulinus. A native of Tanganyika in tropical Africa, this species has small, hooded, clear primrose yellow blooms on 3-foot stems. Its 2½-inch hooded flowers come in clear yellow, orange, pink, red, purple, and violet, as well as white. Bloom is from summer to fall, depending on planting time.

G. tristis. Its 2½ to 3-inch flowers, borne at the top of slender 18-inch stems, are yellow veined with purple, are beautifully fragrant at night, and bloom in March and April.

Another smaller flowered strain, called butterfly gladiolus, has hooded and frilled blooms 3 to 4 inches across, in graceful spikes about as long as those of the large flowered hybrids. They always have at least two colors; this characteristic, not the shape of the flowers, is the reason for its name. You'll find varieties in shades of yellow, apricot, salmon, orange-scarlet, vermilion, poppy red, and creamy white, blotched or lined with deeper or lighter colors. Corms are available in January for planting at the same time as the large flowered hybrids. The butterfly gladiolus, however, will bloom ahead of the big ones.

Use: The gladiolus is a top-ranking cut flower, easy to arrange and long lasting. Baby and miniature gladiolus are charming in informal bouquets; the large flowered hybrids are spectacular in large, formal arrangements. Although often thought of as a second rank landscape plant, if placed in well chosen locations with congenial companions the handsome sword-shaped leaves and richly colored flowers can be an asset. Modern hybrid gladiolus now have sturdy spikes that stand without staking and more flowers per spike.

In garden borders, plant them in groups of one color behind a low hedge or among perennials such as Shasta daisies, dusty miller, gypsophila, or lower Michaelmas daisies; or with annuals such as ageratum, African marigolds, or zinnias.

The smaller gladiolus make fine container plants. This is especially good in cold winter areas, where they can be protected until frosts are over, then moved outside as they come into bud or bloom.

Culture: For top quality blooms on large flowered hybrids, select high-crowned corms at least 1½ inches in diameter. Such corms will produce a single, sturdy stalk with large flowers. Wide flat corms with hollow centers are not as good a buy, since they are older and less vigorous.

Plant corms of large flowered gladiolus as early as possible to avoid damage by thrips. In frostless areas along the Southern California coast, growers of cut flowers plant corms practically every month of the year. However, along most of the California coast, the main planting season is January through March.

In Arizona and other Southwest desert areas, plant between November and February to get blooms before the hot weather. In the Northwest, plant corms in April, May, and June. In the Midwest and the north Atlantic states, the favored planting time is from May through June. In the Southeast plant from April through June.

Plant small flowered gladiolus in fall between September and November. In colder climates, plant as late as possible so that corms will remain dormant during the coldest weather. Set corms 4 inches deep and 4 inches apart.

The ideal environment for gladiolus is in full sun in a light, sandy, rich loam. In inland and desert areas, late-planted gladiolus benefit from light shade.

If your soil is poor, add fertilizer before planting time. Work it in deeply enough so that it will not contact the corms. Use either a complete fertilizer or superphosphate at the rate of 4 pounds for 100 square feet. If you plant in rows, prepare a trench 10 inches deep, incorporate the fertilizer in the bottom, and cover with 4 inches of unfertilized soil.

Set the corms on top of the unfertilized soil with the pointed end facing upward. Depth of planting varies with the size of corm and soil texture. A rule-of-thumb is to plant corms approximately four times their own depth. In light sandy soil, plant large corms 6 inches deep; in heavy soil, set them 3 to 4 inches deep. Plant smaller corms at correspondingly shallower depths. Distance apart also varies with the size of the corm. Set larger corms 6 inches apart; space smaller corms 4 inches apart.

Although gladiolus growing in a good loam or previously enriched soil need little additional fertilizer, some growers recommend a side-dressing of complete fertilizer at the five-leaf stage. Apply it 6 inches from the plants and thoroughly water it in.

About six weeks after blooming, and preferably shortly before the leaves begin to turn yellow, carefully dig the plants with a spading fork. Cut off the stems just above the top of the corm; burn the stems to destroy any thrips that may still be present. Dry

ORNITHOGALUM

RANUNCULUS

RANUNCULUS

RANUNCULUS

corms in a ventilated tray. Place corms in a flat and treat with a bulb dust to destroy any thrip eggs.

Dry the corms in a dry, dark, ventilated place where the temperature remains at 60° to 70°.

When the corms are properly cured (in about three weeks), it will be easy to pull off the old corm and roots from the new plump corm on top. Attached to the new corm may be small, hard-shelled cormels about the size of peas. These may be stored along with the new corms and planted out at the same time next season. It takes two to three years for a cormel to produce flowers.

Discard corms that show signs of disease, indicated by lesions, irregular blotches, or discoloration.

Corms may be stored in single layers in flats or ventilated trays (if you stack containers, place blocks between them to permit air circulation); in paper bags; in shallow boxes with corms covered with dry sand, soil, shavings, or vermiculite; in open-mesh bags; and in paper cartons.

Gloriosa Rothschildiana

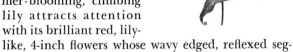

(Glory lily, climbing lily)
Tuber. Tender.

A native of Uganda in tropical Africa, this summer-blooming, climbing lily attracts attention with its brilliant red, lily-like, 4-inch flowers whose wavy edged, reflexed segments are banded with yellow on 6-foot stems.

Use: Grow in containers for a terrace or patio in light shade; pots can also be plunged in the ground, in raised beds, or planter boxes.

Culture: Plant the tuberous roots about 4 inches deep in a horizontal position in light spongy soil. For early bloom, start in pots indoors or in a greenhouse in February. Plant out when the weather becomes warm. Provide wire or a trellis to which the plant can attach itself by means of tendrils at tips of leaves. If the plant is grown indoors, keep the room temperature at 65°. Water growing plants regularly to keep soil moist. Apply liquid fertilizer every three weeks. Withhold water when plants start to go dormant in late fall. When the tops of the plants are dry, you can store the plant in its pot or lift the tuberous roots; treat as dahlias, and repot in early spring.

Glory of the snow, see *Chionodoxa.*

Gloxinia, see *Sinningia speciosa.*

Grape hyacinth, see *Muscari.*

Habranthus

(Rain lily)
Bulb. Semi-hardy.

Habranthus is related to amaryllis and zephyranthes, resembling them in its funnel-shaped blooms, usually appearing one to a stem. Like zephyranthes, habranthus comes into bloom suddenly, after being moistened by rain.

But there are slight differences: the flowers of habranthus are larger than those of zephyranthes, and they are poised at an angle, whereas those of zephyranthes stand upright. Also habranthus' stamens are four different lengths, zephyranthes' are equal.

Although about 20 species of habranthus grow in temperate South America, only a few are commercially available. The two listed below are best known:

H. robustus. The best known habranthus, this Argentinian species has large flowers (3 inches long and 3 inches wide) that are pale pink with deeper pink veining, and green in the throat; stems are 6 to 9 inches tall. Narrow blue-green leaves appear after the flowers.

H. texanus. Sometimes considered a variety of *H. andersonii,* this South American species has naturalized in Texas. Its bright yellow, 1-inch-long flowers with rounded flower segments are coppery, stained with purple on the outside. They bloom in summer on 8-inch stems. Narrow, pointed, blue-green leaves are 4 to 6 inches long.

Use: In milder sections, grow habranthus in sunny borders or rock gardens. If you want to try them outside in colder areas, give them a warm, sheltered position, and provide winter protection. Habranthus are charming pot plants.

Culture: Same as for zephyranthes.

Haemanthus Katherinae

(Blood lily)
Bulb. Tender.

The blood lily is a spectacular South African member of the amaryllis family. It received its name from the red stains on its large (about 4 inches in diameter) white bulb. The plant has three to five broad, wavy-edged, bright green, 12 to 15-inch-long leaves that are nearly ever-green. In early summer, the sturdy 2-foot stalk is topped with a large, ball-like cluster of thin textured, salmon red flowers with myriad thread-like stamens.

Use: This highly individual plant is a superb pot or tub subject in groups or singly in shaded areas.

Culture: Plant a single bulb in a 10-inch pot—or three bulbs in a 14 to 16-inch tub—in January or February. As a soil mix use equal parts of loam and leaf mold or peat moss and add a generous handful per pot of coarse sand or perlite. You can also add 1 tablespoon of bonemeal and 1 teaspoon of blood meal or complete commercial fertilizer for each pot. Set the bulb with the tip even with the soil surface. Water just enough to moisten the soil—until leaves appear. This will take 8 to 10 weeks, during which time the plant should have a 70° day temperature and 50° to 55° at night. In most areas, this means growing the plants indoors.

After leaves develop, water thoroughly and often enough to keep the soil moist. At this point also start feeding once a month with complete liquid fertilizer. In areas where snails are common, apply poison bait; these pests can chew through the stalks. Flowers last longer if protected from the sun during the heat of the day. After bloom, continue watering moderately until fall. Then let the bulb dry out in a cool, dry, but protected place.

Do not disturb the blood lily often. Let the bulb grow in the same pot a second year; simply replace old soil on the top with fresh potting mix. Or, to be more thorough, gently tip the bulb out of the pot, keeping the root ball intact, scrape some soil off sides of the root balls, and repot in a new soil mix. The plants may be increased through the division of well established plants.

Hippeastrum

(Amaryllis)
Bulb. Tender.

While about 70 species of amaryllis grow wild in the southern hemisphere, only a few are available. Most of the amaryllis sold are hybrids.

Remarkably beautiful amaryllis hybrids have been produced both in the United States and in Europe, particularly in Holland. They are available as named varieties in many separate colors. These hybrid strains have impressively large flowers, 8 to 9 inches across and 4 to 6 to a stem, with at least two stems from each bulb. The color range includes exotic reds, salmon, soft pink, and coral pink; there is also a pure white form tinged with green in the throat. They usually flower between February and April; leaves appear after bloom.

Use: Amaryllis, particularly the large-flowered hybrids, are almost always grown in pots. They are also grown outdoors in warm-winter climates.

Culture: Pot bulbs in November or December in rich sandy loam to which bonemeal or a complete commercial fertilizer (1 teaspoon to a 6-inch pot) has been added. The bulbs vary in size; in selecting a pot, allow for 2 inches of space between the bulb and the edge of the pot. Set the bulb so that the neck and one-half of the bulb are above the surface of the soil. Firm soil thoroughly around the base of the bulb and water. Keep soil only slightly moist until the bulb starts to grow, then give it more water.

Keep potted amaryllis in a cool light place at about 50° until roots are well developed; if leaves grow prematurely, the plant may flower poorly, if at all. When leaves appear, increase the temperature to 70°—or up to 75° if you want early bloom. After flower buds form, feed lightly with a complete fertilizer every two weeks throughout the blooming season—1 teaspoon to a 7 or 8-inch pot. After flowers fade, cut off the stem 2 inches above the bulb.

In late summer when the leaves turn yellow, withhold water. In late fall or early winter, when the first signs of growth appear, repot the bulb.

Little bulbs (offsets) on the side of the mother bulb may be left on the bulb, or they may be removed with a piece of root attached and potted up individually to grow on to blooming size in two or three years. You can propagate amaryllis from seeds. Seedlings take three to four years to reach flowering size.

In warm-winter climates, amaryllis can be grown in the garden. With certain precautions, they can also be grown outdoors in colder areas. After frost, either plunge the pot outdoors in the garden or—even better—shift the bulb, with root ball intact, out of the pot and plant it in the ground. Lift in autumn after the first frost and store for the winter in a frost-free place. In areas where the soil does not freeze below 4 inches, the bulbs may be left in the ground (5 inches under the soil surface) and mulched.

Hyacinth

Bulb. Hardy.

About 30 species of hyacinths grow wild in South Africa and the Mediterranean area (Asia Minor, Syria, Greece, and Dalmatia), but only a few—all from the latter region—are cultivated in gardens. Among these are several charming, lesser known, small species and the common hyacinth *(Hyacinthus orientalis)*, from which the well known Dutch hyacinths have been derived.

The hyacinth is closely related to muscari and scilla but differs in that its bell-like flowers are not pinched in tightly at the top, as in muscari. The flower segments of hyacinth are joined for part of their length, rather than being almost completely separated, as in scilla. The intense fragrance of hyacinths is also distinctive.

H. azureus is a delightful species with 8-inch stems which bear nodding, deep blue bells at the bottom of the spike and wide-open, light blue flowers at the top. The erect grooved leaves are bluish green. It blooms in February or March and is excellent for naturalizing. There is also a pure white variety.

H. orientalis (common hyacinth). When compared to the large Dutch forms that have been developed from it, this species is a modest plant. Yet it is an appealing one, which in England and Europe is grown in rock gardens. Its fragrant, bell-shaped flowers in white, pale blue, or purple-blue are loosely spaced on a slender, hollow, 1-foot stem. Basal leaves, as in the larger hyacinths, are thick and strap-shaped.

The Dutch hyacinths—so called because Dutch growers have developed them through extensive cross-breeding and selection—have large, flaring, outward facing bells in tightly crowded spikes on stems up to 18 inches tall. Colors are beautiful and clear: some are delicate pastels of pink, blue, and yellow; others are deep, rich shades of red, royal purple, and dark blue. And there are pure whites.

There also are double-flowered Dutch hyacinths, but they are not as attractive as the single-flowered.

H. orientalis albulus, commonly called the Roman or French Roman hyacinth (native to southern France), is smaller. It has smaller bulbs with white to light blue flowers borne loosely on slender stems; each bulb sends up several stems. Blooming earlier than the Dutch hyacinth, it is less hardy and best adapted to mild-winter areas, such as California and the Southeast. In colder climates it is popular for early forcing indoors.

Hyacinths are graded in Holland according to their circumference measured in centimeters. The largest size bulbs (over 19 centimeters in circumference) are called Exhibition size, and the smallest (14 to 15 centimeters) are called miniatures.

Use: Like larger tulips, the big Dutch hyacinths make impressive displays when massed in beds or borders, particularly if you can afford the luxury of planting them in extensive bands or blocks of graded colors. Strung out in single—or even double—rows, hyacinths look uncomfortably stiff and formal.

By far the most effective and least expensive way to use bedding hyacinths in the average garden is to group one, two, or three dozen bulbs of a single color in a border or at the base of a flowering tree and to skirt the group with a fluffy ground cover of arabis, evergreen candytuft, creeping phlox, or masses of single-colored violas. The ground covers will carry on after the hyacinths have bloomed. You can leave the bulbs in the ground—flowers get smaller in successive years.

Culture: Being deep rooted and heavy feeders, hyacinths grow best in a deep, rich, sandy loam. Fastidious gardeners prepare hyacinth beds as follows: dig trenches a foot or more deep; work a complete fertilizer into the bottom of the trench; over this place 5 to 6 inches of unfertilized soil; set the bulbs 6 to 8 inches apart; and cover with 4 to 6 inches of soil, depending on the size of the bulb.

In cold-winter climates, plant hyacinths in late September to mid October (early enough so that bulbs can establish vigorous roots before the ground freezes). In milder climates, plant hyacinths in October or early November—after the warm days of Indian summer are past. Be sure to keep unplanted bulbs in a cool, dry, dark place.

After bloom, keep watering (unless it rains) until the foliage turns yellow. After the leaves are dry, lift and store the bulbs until fall planting time in a cool, dark, dry place. Or leave the bulbs in the ground and see how they do next spring. To fatten up hyacinth bulbs left in the ground, apply a complete fertilizer and water in after the bloom period.

Hymenocallis Calathina

(Basket flower, spider lily)
Bulb. Tender or semi-hardy.

This South American bulb (sometimes listed as *Ismene calathina*) is also called the Peruvian daffodil because of its resemblance to that flower. The plant forms a basal clump of strap-shaped leaves similar to those of amaryllis. In June and July, strong, smooth, upright, 2-foot stems bear clusters of two to four white, green-striped, daffodil-like blooms with narrow reflexed flower segments. The flowers look as if someone has snipped the edges of the petals in order to improve on nature. Its six stamens are united into a fringed cup with six slender free filaments.

Use: Hymenocallis are worthwhile additions to the summer border, where they combine effectively with such perennials as belladonna, delphiniums, and gypsophila. They are also fine pot or tub plants. All are fragrant and are useful as cut flowers.

Culture: Plant in spring after frosts in rich, well-drained soil. Provide full sun or light shade (in hot summer climates). Set the daffodil-like bulbs with tips just under the surface of the soil; they will bloom a few weeks after planting. Give the plants lots of moisture during the growing season; withhold water after the foliage starts to die down. Lift the bulbs before severe cold sets in and bury them in dry sand or vermiculite in a dry place at a temperature of 70°. Be sure bulbs are dry before storing.

Ipheion Uniflorum

(Spring star flower)
Bulb. Hardy.

A native of Argentina that formerly was called *Brodiaea uniflora* and *Triteleia uniflora,* this is the familiar plant with flattish, bluish green leaves that smell like onions. Each flower at the top of 6 to 8-inch-high stems is 1¼ to 1½ inches wide, white, tinged with darker blue, the undersides veined with bluish-brown. It blooms in spring.

Use: Like brodiaeas, these plants perform best in out-of-the-way garden places that need little water in summer. When planted in older gardens as an edging, they seem to take garden conditions with ease.

Culture: Performs best in sandy or gritty soil. They need moisture during the growing season but should dry off completely in summer. Plant corms 2 to 3 inches deep. In severe-winter climates, protect with a thick mulch of leaves or straw.

Iris

Rhizome or bulb. Hardy.

Native to nearly every country in the northern hemisphere, irises can be found that will be suited to almost every kind of soil and climate. They are remarkably diverse in flower colors and forms, in blooming seasons, and in cultural requirements. Learning to know even a portion of this large group could occupy a lifetime — and provide no end of fascination.

Irises are divided into three main groups: bearded, beardless, and crested. The bearded and crested sorts grow from rhizomes; many of the beardless ones do, too, but some of them grow instead from true bulbs.

Bearded Irises

Contained in this group are the most familiar garden irises. Four types fall into this category: tall bearded, median bearded, dwarf bearded, and the aril species with their hybrids, the arilbreds.

Tall Bearded. Mention iris and this is the type that usually comes to mind. They've been around for centuries but have undergone a rapid evolution at the hands of hybridizers in this century. Today's tall bearded irises are magnificent plants — 2½ to 4 feet tall with branched stems bearing beautifully formed flowers of excellent substance and texture in a kaleidoscopic color range (all except true red and green).

These irises are adapted to a wide range of climates except for most of the area from South Carolina through the South to eastern Texas, where summer rains and high humidity prevent proper ripening of rhizomes. They require well drained and nearly neutral soil. Except for leafspot and iris borer (and this only east of the Rocky Mountains), they are comparatively free from diseases and pests.

Median Irises. This classification includes several types of smaller bearded irises, many of which boast tall beardeds in their ancestry. All require the same culture as tall beardeds. Border bearded irises are the short offspring from regular tall bearded iris. Bloomstalks are 15 to 28 inches tall and flowers are somewhat smaller than tall beardeds; bloom season is the same. Miniature tall bearded irises (formerly table irises) have small (2½ to 3½ inches across), airy blossoms on branching, pencil-slim stems 15 to 25 inches high. They differ from border beardeds and intermediate bearded irises in that all plant parts are more dainty. Intermediate bearded irises usually are hybrids between tall beardeds and dwarf sorts, and their bloom season falls between that of the tall beardeds and the miniature dwarfs. Though stems are 15 to 28 inches high, their blooms reflect the colors and style of tall beardeds. In contrast to border beardeds, the intermediates generally have a smaller overall appearance and are more prolific. Standard dwarf beardeds (the final median category) generally are hybrids of tall beardeds and miniature dwarfs. These reach peak bloom on 10 to 15-inch slightly branched stems three weeks to a month before the tall beardeds. These are excellent plants for early spring borders: increase is rapid, and the flowers (which appear just above the leaves) are abundant.

Miniature Dwarf Bearded Irises. Elves of the iris world (3 to 10 inches high), these are the earliest bearded irises to flower. They come in jewel-like colors: blue, yellow, brilliant orange, purple, violet, almost black, red-brown, pure white—even green. Blossoms may be satin smooth or velvety, often with a contrasting spot on the falls. Nearly all require winter chilling below 32° to grow well.

Aril and Arilbred Irises. This group, comprising Oncocyclus and Regelia irises and their hybrids, is more important for the part some members have played in hybridizing than for their performance as individual garden plants. The term "aril" refers to the white collar on the seeds of all of this group's species. Oncocyclus irises have only one large flower to each stalk, often very large, globular, and intricately patterned, with broad, diffused beards.

Instead of being large and rounded, regelia flowers are smaller and elongated, two to each stem, with long, narrow beards. The two types have been hybridized to give a group of named hybrids (collectively called Oncogelias) intermediate in appearance and easier to grow than either parent.

Arilbred irises are the result of hybridizers trying to combine the unique colors, patterns, and flower forms of aril species with the ease of growth and better stems and foliage of tall bearded and median irises. Many of these have strikingly beautiful blooms on plants nearly as easy to grow as tall beardeds. In the arid Southwest, most need no special care. In other parts of the country, they prefer slightly alkaline soil with good drainage.

Uses for Bearded Irises. In smaller gardens, the most effective way to use irises is to plant them in clumps of separate colors in mixed flower borders. In mixed plantings, be careful not to interplant with anything that crowds or shades the rhizomes since this can lead to rhizome rot.

Culture of Bearded Irises. Sunshine is necessary to get flowers; in deep shade, irises produce only leaves. Sun for half the day is sufficient in warm interior climates, but they need full sun in cooler coastal areas. Drainage is extremely important; if the site is not naturally well drained, plant in beds raised 4 to 6 inches above normal grade.

Clumps of irises give their best bloom in the second and third years, often fair in the fourth. After that time, increase of new rhizomes and a network of old ones result in overcrowded conditions with insufficient food supply for all. Then it's time to dig and separate the clumps, but wait at least six weeks after bloom before you begin to dig. Save the strongest rhizomes for replanting, cutting their leaves back to about 6 inches to help compensate for root loss.

Best times for planting are from about July 1 through September. Plant earlier in this period in cold climates, later where summers are hot. Ideally, have the soil prepared a few weeks or more in advance of planting: spade in generous quantities of organic materials (even manures if you wait at least a month to plant), a sprinkling of commercial bulb fertilizer or bonemeal, and—if your soil is heavy clay—a snowlike dusting of gypsum. Plant single rhizomes at least a foot apart, with tops of rhizomes *just* beneath the soil surface. New growth comes from the end where the leaves are, so point the leafy end in the direction you want growth to take. If you plant several in clump formation, face the leafy ends outward to avoid quick overcrowding.

Autumn care consists of removing all brown, dried leaves and any debris that may have accumulated in the bed. Where soil is likely to freeze or alternately freeze and thaw, apply a winter mulch.

From early spring and continuing through the flowering season, be sure to water your iris plantings regularly. After they flower, continue to irrigate weekly for about another month while next year's flower buds are being formed. In hot summer areas, irrigate at least every other week.

Best fertilizers are those relatively low in nitrogen and high in phosphorus and potash. Too much nitrogen encourages lush, soft growth that is more susceptible to foliage and rhizome diseases; flowers will be fewer, too. Give plants a light application in early spring as growth starts and after flowering.

Bearded irises have few pests and diseases. Rhizome rot, a bacterial disease, occurs occasionally during the bloom season and during summer, whenever too much water and heat are present. In severe cases, dig up the infected plants and scrape out the soft parts. Then either immerse the rhizomes in liquid chlorine bleach (1 part in 10 parts water) or paint full strength bleach on the scraped area or liberally dust with gypsum. Leave rhizomes exposed to air for several days before replanting. If you replant in the same location, replace the soil with soil from another part of the garden. In less severe cases, pull soil away from infected rhizomes, scrape and cut out all soft parts, paint rhizomes with the bleach, and leave cut rhizome surfaces exposed to the air. Where iris borer is a problem, spray with sevin or diazinon before the blooming season.

Beardless Irises

Included in this group are species that lack beards and have generally narrower flower parts than do most bearded sorts. The first group contains those beardless irises that grow from rhizomes. The second group contains beardless sorts that grow from bulbs.

BEARDLESS IRISES WITH RHIZOMES. In contrast to the bearded irises, many of these beardless sorts prefer a moist to actually wet soil during the growing season. All are more difficult to transplant because their roots must not dry out during the process.

Japanese Irises. Their large flat flowers bring the iris season to a glorious climax in July, offering a rich tapestry of purples, blues, pinks, and white. There are single and double-flowered varieties. This iris grows to perfection in rich, slightly acid soil, with ample water. Light shade is preferable in warmer areas. The worst enemy of Japanese iris is alkalinity; counteract it with applications of acid-base fertilizers. Plant in late summer or early fall in colder sections to permit plants to get well established before winter. You can also plant them in early spring. Many gardeners plant Japanese iris in boxes or large pots and submerge them in ponds or shallow pools during the growing season. Lift and drain the containers in late fall and keep the plants dry in winter.

Louisiana Irises. From four species found in the lower Mississippi River valley have been produced hybrids with flowers in pure white, yellow, pink, red, purple, and a complete range of blue shades—nearly all with a contrasting spear of yellow on each sepal. Louisiana irises are adaptable to colder (but not the coldest) areas, as well as to warmer, drier climates. Provide a slightly acid soil, amply supplied with peat moss or leaf mold, and give them plenty of water. Although the species often grow in standing water, the hybrids perform surprisingly well with normal garden watering. Plant in filtered shade in warmer sections, in full sun in cooler climates.

Pacific Coast Irises. A number of species native to open woodlands and coastal meadows of California, Oregon, and Washington can be grown easily in their native states. Nearly all require excellent drainage (the exception being *I. douglasiana* and its hybrids) and lightly filtered summer sun where summers are hot (in cool coastal areas, they will take full sun). Many of the species come in a wide color range; and where two or more overlap their ranges in nature, many unusual natural hybrids may be found. The most commonly sold species are *I. douglasiana*, *I. innominata*, and *I. tenax*. Hybridizers have taken the most attractive species and produced many beautiful named hybrids noted for their graceful flower forms and striking color patterns. Heights range from 1 to 2 feet.

Siberian Irises. Pale to deep blue, purple, purplish red, or white butterfly-like flowers on 2 to 4-foot stems bloom just as the late tall bearded irises are beginning to fade. The narrow leaves, shorter than the flower stems, form thick clumps that need infrequent dividing (about every 8 to 10 years); divide in September and cover rhizomes with 2 inches of soil. Plant Siberians in full sun. Although they prefer a slightly acid soil, they will thrive in ordinary soil along with most kinds of perennials if given an application of acid fertilizer annually in spring.

Spuria Irises. Popularly called "butterfly irises," the name gives a clue to their graceful flower form and carriage but not a hint of the extraordinary petal toughness. Colors range from white through cream and yellow, light bronze to chocolate brown, all shades of blue and lavender, and combinations of several colors—often attractively veined and usually with a small to large yellow patch on the falls. In some new hybrids, flowers are as large as the average tall bearded. Plants are fans of narrow, erect foliage 2 to 3½ feet high; they form compact clumps that can remain undivided for five to eight years or more. Bloom is in late spring, beginning with the late tall beardeds. Three conditions must be met for success with Spurias: warm to hot summers, good drainage, and scant summer moisture. Bloom is not plentiful in cool climates, and moist soil in hot weather promotes attacks by mustard seed rot (to guard against this, mix powdered 75 per cent pentachloronitrobenzene into the soil when planting). Plant rhizomes, or divide old clumps, in fall—late fall where winters are mild—and keep plants moist until they are established. Cover rhizomes with about 1 inch of soil. The best soil for them is well drained and neutral, containing plenty of organic matter. Where winters are definitely cold, mulch as you would tall bearded irises. Give them ample moisture during the spring growing season and until bloom stops; fertilize in early spring and fall.

BEARDLESS IRISES FROM BULBS. Far fewer in number than the rhizomatous beardless irises, this group nevertheless includes two cut-flower favorites and a familiar rock garden subject.

Dutch Irises. Descendants or variations of the Spanish iris (*I. xiphium*), the Dutch irises have almost entirely replaced the ancestor from which they were derived. (They are called Dutch only because they were hybridized in Holland.) Orchid-like flowers come in superb colors with firm substance; they have long, strong, straight stems and are long-lasting cut flowers. Bloom is in March and April in mild winter areas, in May and June in colder sections.

Plant in sun, setting bulbs 4 inches deep and 3 to 4 inches apart in well-drained soil. Give lots of water when in growth. Although the bulbs are hardy, winter top growth may be frozen in severe winters unless protected with straw, hay, or evergreen boughs. Remove the tops as you would gladiolus and store the bulbs in a cool, dry place until time to plant but not more than two months. Dutch irises are splendid container plants; pot in October, placing five bulbs in a 5 or 6-inch pot, with the bulb tip just below the surface of the soil.

Reticulata Irises. These are the earliest bulbous irises to bloom—often in January in milder sections, in March or April in colder climates. The name "reticulata" comes from the word *reticulate*, meaning netted, and refers to the finely netted covering of the bulbs. Several species and named selections are sold in colors of blue, purple, violet, yellow, or white, usually with yellow markings on the falls. The tallest of them reach only about 6 inches. Reticulatas need a good but gritty soil with excellent drainage.

Crested Irises. These dainty irises are more closely related to bearded irises than to the beardless kinds. The distinguishing characteristic of this group is a small linear crest at the base of the falls. Unlike most irises, these will accept a good deal of shade.

I. cristata. This native of America is an enchanting miniature with broad, short leaves (4 to 6 inches) and elfin-like, lavender flowers with golden crests. It blooms in April or May. Provide a cool, damp soil, light shade.

I. gracilipes. A Japanese species. Several small, lavender flowers, about an inch across, grow on slender branched stems 8 to 10 inches tall. Provide a moist, well drained soil containing ample humus. Not hardy in cold climates.

I. tectorum. This iris is called "roof iris" because for years it has been planted on thatched roof ridges in Japan. Broad, ribbed leaves are about 1 foot tall; flowers are purple-blue with white crests or pure white. This species is best adapted to climates with moist atmosphere.

I. japonica. Sometimes called the "orchid iris" because its delicate, graceful blooms are reminiscent of that flower, this iris has widely branched, 2-foot stems which bear pale lavender, fringed flowers with orange crests. Plant in light shade. This species is adapted only to milder climates; in the Midwest and Northeast, grow *I. japonica* in pots in a greenhouse.

Ixia Maculata

(African corn lily)
Corm. Tender or semi-hardy.

Although there are 25 to 30 species of ixias, only a few are widely cultivated; most popular and generally available is the species *I. maculata.* The upper third of its graceful, wiry, 18 to 20-inch stems are topped in May and June with spike-like clusters of 1 to 2-inch cup-shaped flowers in cream, yellow, orange, red, and pink shades—all with darker centers.

Use: Flower arrangers appreciate the ixia's gaily colored blooms that last about two weeks after being cut. In mild-winter areas, ixias are effective in borders by themselves or with ground covers, such as the perennial snow-in-summer *(Cerastium)* or the annual sweet alyssum. Where winters are too severe for outdoor culture, ixias may be grown indoors in pots. On dull days and at night, the flowers close, but they open up widely in sunshine or when they are brought into the warmth of the house.

Culture: In mild sections, plant corms in early fall, setting them 3 inches deep and 2 to 3 inches apart in full sun in sandy well drained soil. In western Oregon and Washington, plant after November 1, placing corms 4 inches deep. If you expect frosts, plant corms in sheltered position and apply a protective mulch. In mild climates, ixias increase freely by seeding themselves in beds that are not watered in summer.

To grow in a pot, plant six to eight corms 1 inch deep in a 5-inch pot in a mixture of sandy loam and peat moss or leaf mold. Place in a coldframe or other cool shaded place where corms can develop roots. Water very lightly until root forms. When leaves appear, admit light and increase watering. As buds start to form, move pots into a sunny place but not into too much heat. If you grow potted ixias indoors you will get better flowers if temperatures are held between 40° to 50°. After flowering, withhold watering gradually. When foliage is dry, clean the corms and store them as you do gladiolus.

Lachenalia

(Cape cowslip)
Bulb. Tender.

Versatile but comparatively little known, these South African bulbs bloom for six to eight weeks in late winter and early spring. The following two species (out of a total of 50 that grow wild) are most often grown as house plants.

L. bulbifera (L. pendula) displays spikes of 1½-inch, red and yellow, purple-tipped, tubular flowers on thick, fleshy, 1-foot stems. Succulent leaves, 2 inches across, are similar in shape to those of tulips.

L. tricolor has yellow flowers with inner segments tipped with red, the outer segments are tipped with green. The 1-inch-wide leaves are often spotted with purple or dark green.

Use: Grow as a pot plant in the house in severe climates. In warm-winter areas, it may be grown in borders, rock gardens, window boxes, raised beds. Lachenalias also make interesting hanging basket plants and are good cut flowers.

Culture: Plant bulbs in summer and fall. To grow in pots, put six bulbs in a 5 or 6-inch pot in loamy soil, setting them with the tips just under the surface. Keep the potted bulbs in a cool, dimly lit place—perhaps a coldframe—until roots form. When leaves appear, provide more warmth (50° night temperature) and plenty of water. Light applications of liquid fertilizer are beneficial after the flower spikes show. When flowers and leaves start withering, gradually reduce watering. Keep the plants quite dry until August or early September, when it will be time to repot the bulbs in fresh soil. Lachenalia bulbs multiply rapidly, and small bulblets can be sown in flats or pots for next season's bloom. In frostless areas, grow lachenalias in sunny borders. If you lift them carefully, you can shift the plants from the ground into pots while they are in full bloom.

Leucocoryne Ixioides

(Glory-of-the-sun)
Bulb. Semi-hardy.

An intriguing Chilean native, glory-of-the-sun was first introduced to the United States from England in the early 1930s by seed. It received considerable publicity and bulbs were quite widely available in the few years following but are now difficult to find. They are still worth seeking out, however, for the sake of the almost legendary beauty and fragrance of their flowers, especially the variety 'Odorata'. Waxy, sweet-scented, brodiaea-like, lavender-blue, 2-inch blooms with white centers are borne in clusters on slender, wiry, 12 to 18-inch stems in mid-spring. Leaves are grass-like.

Use: This bulb is best suited for rock gardens or for naturalizing in sections of the garden that need not be watered in the summer. It can be grown with South African bulbs, such as freesias, ixias, sparaxis, and tritonias. It is also a splendid flower for arrangements, remaining fresh for two weeks or more. The flowers are lovely and waxy with a delightful fragrance.

Culture: Plant bulbs in fall, 3 inches deep and 5 inches apart, in sunny well-drained spots in mild-winter areas. In colder sections, plant bulbs in pots in the same way as freesias. Provide ample moisture during the growing and blooming periods, but let the bulbs dry out in summer. The bulbs have a tendency to move downward in the soil; some gardeners try planting them in containers or in beds with fine wire mesh stretched across the bottom. One grower suggests that a layer of stiff clay at the bottom of the bed helps to impede the bulbs' subterranean movement—but only on slopes where excess water can drain off readily.

These plants can be grown from seed; the bulbs do not increase by division.

Leucojum

(Snowflake)
Bulb. Hardy

Gardeners understandably confuse the closely related snowflakes and snowdrops *(Galanthus)*. Their bulbs look alike, both have strap-shaped leaves, and at first glance their white, green-tipped, bell-shaped flowers are almost identical in appearance.

But there are some important differences. Snowdrops always bear only one flower to a stem, and the inner segments overlap so they appear tubular, whereas most species of snowflake carry two or more flowers to stem, and the perianth segments are distinctly separate. Snowdrop bulbs usually produce only two leaves, rarely three; each snowflake bulb puts out several leaves.

Snowdrops are much better suited to cold winters and often die out the second year in warmer climates; snowflakes, on the other hand, seem to grow well under both conditions.

L. aestivum is commonly called the summer snowflake, a name that hardly fits its blooming period. In the warmer sections of the West, this species often blooms in late November and continues into the winter months. It flowers along with narcissus in the Northwest, in May along the Atlantic Coast.

Leaves are 12 to 18 inches long; each stem, as long or longer than the leaves, carries three to five pendulous, white, bell-shaped flowers whose six pointed segments are jauntily dotted with bright green.

L. vernum, the spring snowflake, bears its single flower, similar to those of the summer snowflake, on 12-inch stems. The bright green, glossy leaves are 9 inches long. In the East, it comes into bloom in late winter or very early spring while the snowdrops are still in flower. It also makes its appearance far ahead of the spring season in warmer parts of the country, and as early as January in the Northwest.

Use: Snowflakes naturalize nicely under high branching deciduous trees where the winter sun shines through freely. In older gardens you often find them in masses along back fences or walls.

Culture: Plant bulbs with the tip 4 inches under the surface of the soil. They thrive under the same conditions as daffodils. Bulbs increase readily and can remain undisturbed for several years. A new planting takes two seasons to develop properly. When the flowers dwindle in size and number, lift the clumps (after the foliage dies down in summer), separate the bulbs, and replant immediately in thoroughly prepared soil. Like galanthus, bulbs of *L. vernum* must be stored in damp peat moss.

SCILLA PERUVIANA   TIGRIDIA

TRITONIA   ZANTEDESCHIA

Lilium

(Lily)
Bulb. Hardy.

Lilies are truly among the aristocrats of the floral kingdom. They have been cultivated in gardens for centuries, but until quite recently only native species were available — plants exactly like those that grow in the wild in Asia, Europe, and North America. Now hybridists, using species with desirable qualities, have produced hybrid lilies that are healthier, hardier, and easier to grow. These new hybrids are remarkably varied and handsome in form and color, providing a succession of bloom from May to October.

True lilies are members of the genus *Lilium* and are quite different from other so-called "lily" plants. The Royal Horticultural Society of England and the North American Lily Society have established a system of classification. These are the most widely available lilies in North America:

ASIATIC HYBRIDS. The Upright Flowering forms are derived from such species as *L. tigrinum*, *L. cernuum*, *L. davidii*, *L. dauricum*, *L. amabile*, *L. maculatum*, and *L. bulbiferum*. They are early flowering lilies with upright flowers, borne singly or in clusters. Examples: Mid-Century Hybrids, 'Enchantment,' 'Pirate,' 'Nova,' and 'Golden Chalice.'

The Outward-Facing Asiatic Hybrids are derived from the same parents as the upright. Examples: 'Prosperity,' 'Paprika,' and 'Corsage.'

The Pendant Flowering Asiatics are hybrids of *L. amabile*, *L. cernuum*, *L. davidii*, and *L. tigrinum*. These lilies are notable for their hardiness and vigor. Examples: 'Citronella,' 'Harlequin Hybrids,' 'Amber Gold,' 'Sonata,' and Hallmark Strain.

MARTAGON HYBRIDS. From parentage of *L. martagon* and *L. hansonii*, this plant has a wide range of colors and graceful forms, such as the Paisley Hybrids. The recurved flowers are available in rich warm shades of yellow, orange, lilac, purple, tangerine, and mahogany. Martagon Hybrids bloom in June

AMERICAN HYBRIDS. Hybrids of North American species, *L. humboldtii*, *L. kelloggii*, *L. pardalinum*, and *L. parryi*, this group includes a wide range of colors and forms, and is often fragrant. These hybrids naturalize well and bloom in late June or early July. Examples: Bellingham Hybrids, San Gabriel Strain, 'Shuksan,' 'Buttercup,' and 'Robin.'

AURELIAN HYBRIDS. The parent species of the Chinese Trumpet Aurelian Hybrids, *L. centifolium*, *L. henryi*, *L. regale*, and *L. sargentiae*, have provided a wide range of color in these funnel shaped lilies. Flowers appear in July and August. Examples: 'Pink Perfection,' 'Golden Splendor,' 'Green Magic,' and 'Black Dragon.'

The Bowl-Shaped Aurelian Hybrids are derived from *L. sargentiae*, *L. sulphureum*, and *L. henryi*. Examples: 'First Love' and 'Heart's Desire.'

The Sunburst Aurelian Hybrids are derived from *L. centifolium*, *L. henryi*, *L. sargentiae*, *L. regale*, and others. These vigorous and hardy plants are particularly suitable for colder climates. Examples: 'Golden Sunburst' and 'Thunderbolt.'

ORIENTAL HYBRIDS. This group of hybrids of *L. auratum*, *L. speciosum*, *L. japonicum*, and *L. rubellum*, includes crosses with *L. henryi*. They generally flower in August. There are Bowl-Shaped Oriental Hybrids exemplified by 'Empress of India,' 'Red Baron,' 'Pink Glory,' and 'Crimson Beauty.'

The Flat-Faced Oriental Hybrids are derived from parents native to Japan, include *L. auratum* (Gold Band Lily), *L. speciosum* (Rubrum Lily), and the pink *L. japonicum*. Examples: the Imperial Strains. (Crimson, Silver, and Gold).

The Recurved Oriental Hybrids come from the most exotic and strong growing lilies native to Japan, China, and Formosa (Taiwan) including *L. auratum* and *L. speciosum*. Examples: 'Jamboree,' 'Allegra,' 'Grand Commander,' and 'Red Champion.'

EASTER LILIES. *L. longiflorum* (white trumpet lily) is the most widely recognized species lily. It is frequently forced to bloom at Easter. Treatment of Easter lilies: as soon as the last flower fades, transplant your gift Easter lily to a sunny or partially shady spot in the garden with good drainage. It may bloom again that fall. After adjusting to its new environment in a year or two, it will flower in midsummer (its normal blooming time).

SPECIES LILIES AND THEIR VARIETIES. Included in this list are many of the species and varieties that have been in cultivation for a long time. They are native to Asia, Europe, Japan, and North America.

Following are the lilies of foreign origin:

L. auratum 'Platyphyllum'. This is the gold-band lily whose waxy white, fragrant flowers are spotted with crimson and display a golden band down the center of each segment. It grows 4 to 6 feet high and blooms in August and early September.

L. candidum. This pure white lily has been grown for thousands of years. Bulbs must be planted in August, shortly after foliage from the previous season's growth dies down. Set bulb with only 1 to 2 inches of soil over the top.

L. formosanum pricei. White, narrow, trumpet-shaped flowers bloom in June, July on 18-inch stems.

L. formosanum wilsonii. Last of the lilies to bloom, having white trumpet flowers. (In milder climates, blooms as late as December.) Plant the small bulbs 5 to 6 inches deep to insure heavy stem roots.

L. martagon. Turk's cap or martagon lily. This

PA HAGARI

PA FOSTERIANA

TULIPA (COTTAGE)

TULIPA KAUFMANNIANA

TULIPA (DARWIN)

European species has pink, recurved, pendant flowers on 3 to 5-foot stems. It is difficult to establish, but after two years in congenial surroundings, it forms large clumps and continues indefinitely. *L. m.* 'Album,' pure white form, is one of the most appealing of all lilies. Blooms in June and July.

L. nepalense 'Robustum'. Uniquely beautiful soft green flowers with maroon centers bloom in July and August on stems 1 to 1½ feet high.

L. pumilum, formerly called *L. tenuifolium,* with the common name of coral lily. Wiry 2-foot stems bear bright scarlet flowers.

L. regale. Although now superseded in quality and vigor by modern hybrid strains ('Black Dragon' and 'Green Magic'), the regal lily is still one of the most popular and widely sold trumpet lilies. The white flowers bloom in June and July.

L. speciosum 'Rubrum'. Showy red lily, prized for garden, cutting, and containers. Bulbs require two years to become well established. It grows 2½ to 3½ feet high. *L.s.* 'Black Beauty' with deep crimson flowers, is an extremely vigorous plant that grows over 5 feet high. *L.s.* 'Album,' a pure white form grows 2½ to 4 feet. All bloom in August and September.

These are West Coast natives:

L. columbianum. Columbia lily. Nodding reflexed flowers are bright orange with large maroon dots, on 2 to 4-foot-high stems. It grows wild in northern California, through Oregon, Washington, western Idaho, and southern British Columbia.

L. humboldtii. Humboldt lily. A native of open woodlands in the Sierra Nevada Mountains in central California. Similar to, but larger (3 to 6 feet high) than *L. columbianum.*

L. pardalinum. The well-known leopard lily of California. Recurved Turk's cap blooms are bright crimson near the tips and brown-spotted.

Following are Eastern native lilies:

L. canadense. Called the meadow lily, this native grows from Nova Scotia to Georgia and Alabama. Bell-shaped orange-yellow to crimson-red flowers bloom on 2 to 5-foot stems in July.

L. superbum. American Turk's cap lily. A colorful lily with orange, maroon-spotted flowers, native from eastern Massachusetts to southern Indiana and south to northwestern Florida and Alabama.

Use: Everything about a well grown lily suggests a noble plant: the proud manner in which flower clusters stand out on strong stems, the clean lines of trumpet or chalice-shaped blooms, the rich colors.

Clumps of tall lilies can grow for many years in generous spaces between shrubs and low growing evergreens in partially shaded borders. Their finest companions include azaleas, camellias, *Cocculus laurifolius,* hydrangeas, kalmia, *Osmanthus delavayii.*

There is almost no limit to the number of combinations in which you can use lilies in perennial borders. With the full complement of heights, form, and blooming periods available in modern lily hybrids, it is possible to find varieties for the foreground, middle distance, and the background.

You can use lilies to provide a summer follow-up to spring flowering blubs. After the earlier blooming bulbs fade, set out non-invasive annuals, such as petunias or *Phlox drummondii,* to carpet the ground.

Lilies are superb container plants. For information on how to grow them this way, see page 10.

When treated properly, lilies can hardly be surpassed for sheer beauty and long life in indoor arrangements. Take care in handling pollen-laden lily flowers. Moist, fresh pollen stains the flowers and clothing, too. Once the pollen is completely dry, you can brush it off quite easily, without leaving a smudge.

Culture: Lilies thrive in a porous, moist, rich soil that is neutral or slightly acid (a pH of 5.5 to 6.5 is preferred); a few, such as the Madonna and martagon lilies, will grow in the presence of lime. If soil needs enriching, work in complete fertilizer before planting or apply it around the plants after they have produced several inches of top growth. Good drainage is essential for lilies. Bulbs rot in soggy soil.

In cool coastal areas, grow lilies in full sun; high filtered shade is preferable where summers are hot.

Lilies never go completely dormant. Plant the bulbs as soon as possible after receiving them. Handle carefully, since the bulb scales are soft and bruise easily. If bulbs appear dried out, place them in moist sand or peat moss in a cool spot until scales become firm and plump and roots appear; then plant them.

Planting depths vary according to the rooting habit of the bulbs: base-rooting types are planted more shallowly than those which produce roots on the stems above the bulbs.

Make generous planting holes; place loose, well prepared soil in the bottom, set the bulb, carefully spreading its roots, then fill over it with soil. Some gardeners set lily bulbs on 1 or 2 inches of sand.

In severe winter climates, apply a mulch of light, non-packing material over lily beds after the first freeze. The mulch will prevent alternate freezing and thawing of the soil and help to keep down weeds. In hot summer areas, mulches are extremely helpful in keeping the soil cool around the bulbs.

Since lily bulbs never stop growing, they need a constant supply of moisture. Soak thoroughly to a depth of at least 6 inches; avoid sprinkling the foliage, since this encourages spread of disease spores.

During the growing season, watch for aphids. If these insects attack your lilies, spray with the same insecticide you use for your roses. One sure way to get virus-free lilies is to grow them from seed. The virus dies with the bulb.

After lilies are well established in congenial surroundings, they will increase in beauty and number.

Lift and divide clumps only after one year's bloom is less than the previous year's and flowers and stalks get noticeably smaller. The best time to do this is in fall after the leaves and stems turn yellow.

Lycoris

(Spider lily)
Bulb. Tender or semi-hardy.

Lycoris is the Asian counterpart of nerine, a South African bulb which it closely resembles. Narrow, strap-shaped, basal leaves appear in spring and shortly after start ripening, dying down completely in late summer. Soon after leaves are gone, solid, smooth stems emerge and rapidly grow up to 2 feet; in August or September they are topped with clusters of red, pink, or yellow flowers with narrow, pointed, wavy-edged, recurved segments and long exserted stamens that contribute a spidery appearance.

L. aurea. Called the golden spider lily, it produces bright yellow, iridescent, 3-inch flowers after the blue-green leaves disappear. Give this tender bulb a protected spot.

L. radiata. This best known and most easily grown spider lily has deep pink to nearly scarlet blooms with a gold sheen; stems are 18 inches tall. The variety 'Alba' has white flowers and will take light shade. With protection, *L. radiata* can be grown outside in western Oregon and Washington.

L. squamigera (Amaryllis hallii). Commonly called hardy amaryllis, naked ladies, or hurricane lily. Fragrant pink or rosy lilac, 3-inch blooms appear in August on 2-foot stems.

Use: These striking plants are well suited for pots, making interesting accents on terraces and patios. All may be grown outdoors in milder sections; *L. squamigera* may be planted in borders in colder areas, where it will winter over without mulching.

Culture: Plant bulbs in late summer or fall in sandy loam with humus added. Set bulbs of *L. aurea* and *L. radiata* 3 or 4 inches deep. The large bulbs of *L. squamigera* (2 or 3 inches in diameter) should be planted 6 inches deep. During the active growing period, provide both potted and garden-grown lycoris with ample water. Remember that it is highly important to see that they are thoroughly dried out during the dormant period in summer. Avoid disturbing bulbs for several years. When potting bulbs, set them with the tops exposed; don't use too large pots, since the bulbs flower more profusely when roots are crowded.

Milla Biflora

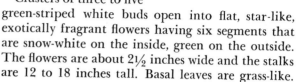

(Mexican star)
Bulb. Semi-hardy.

Exuding a Southwestern charm, this low-growing plant is native to Arizona, New Mexico, and Mexico.
Clusters of three to five green-striped white buds open into flat, star-like, exotically fragrant flowers having six segments that are snow-white on the inside, green on the outside. The flowers are about 2½ inches wide and the stalks are 12 to 18 inches tall. Basal leaves are grass-like.

Use: Millas are most effective in sunny borders and rock gardens, as edgings, and in pots. They are good plants for the small garden.

Culture: Set out bulbs in October in a sunny location in light, perfectly drained soil. In warm, sheltered locations with a protective mulch, millas have survived winters on the East Coast as far north as New York City. Plant several bulbs in a pot for late winter and early spring bloom in a cool greenhouse or in a sunny window indoors.

Muscari

(Grape hyacinth)
Bulb. Hardy.

For their welcome blue in spring, their hardy, easy-going constitution, and ability to grow in almost any soil, grape hyacinths rate as favorites practically everywhere. Although closely related to the common hyacinth (*Hyacinthus*), these smaller bulbs differ in these ways: muscari's bells are pinched in at the lower end, whereas the hyacinth's flower segments are flaring or reflexed; and leaves of grape hyacinth are generally grass-like and more fleshy. The fact that the foliage appears in autumn worries some gardeners in cold climates, but it is rarely damaged by low temperatures.

M. armeniacum jauntily bears brilliant blue, fragrant bells in tight clusters on 4 to 8-inch stems rising above longer, floppy leaves.

M. botryoides (in Latin, botryoides means "like a bunch of grapes"), the common grape hyacinth and once most frequently grown and widely available. Deep blue flowers appear on 6 to 12-inch stems. A charming white variety, 'Album,' is less readily available.

M. comosum, the fringe or tassel hyacinth, carries its odd, shredded looking flowers on 8 to 12-inch, brown-spotted stems. Blooms are borne in a branched compact cluster. It is somewhat difficult to grow.

M. tubergenianum, an exquisite, two-toned blue species from northwestern Persia, is often referred to as Oxford and Cambridge grape hyacinth. The bells at the top of the 8-inch stalk are dark (Oxford) blue, while those at the bottom are lighter (Cambridge) blue. This species does not produce untidy foliage.

Use: Grape hyacinths are wonderful for sheets of blue under spring blooming trees and deciduous shrubs. But they are not for the gardener who resents the sight of fading foliage that must inevitably follow the bloom. For such gardeners, the best place to grow muscari is on the outskirts of the garden or in containers.

Culture: Plant bulb 2 inches deep in sun in any well drained garden soil. In warmer climates, grape hyacinths will perform satisfactorily in light shade under trees, or in an east exposure. Under favorable conditions, grape hyacinths increase readily and can become a problem in mixed borders or rock gardens. Lift and divide the bulbs when they become crowded.

Narcissus

(Daffodils, Jonquils)
Bulb. Hardy.

If you could have only one kind of bulb in your garden, you would probably choose the daffodil (*Narcissus*), like most of the world's gardeners. These cheerful, reliable bulbs, which grow wild in central Europe, the Mediterranean region, and east to China and Japan, have almost no end of virtues.

• They are permanent, increasing from year to year.
• They flower regularly and profusely with a fascinating variety of flower forms and colors and provide a long sequence of bloom.
• They are hardy to cold and can stand summer heat.
• They are adapted to many different garden situations—from sun-baked hillsides to filtered woodland shade, to banks of pools and streams. You can grow them as container plants on terraces and patios.
• The bitter taste of their bulbs repels such common marauders as pocket gophers, chipmunks, ground squirrels, and mice.

We use daffodil as a common name for all members of the genus *Narcissus.* Many gardeners mistakenly use the term daffodil interchangeably with jonquil—one species of narcissus, specifically *N. jonquilla.* Still others think of the trumpet-flowered varieties as daffodils and the small-cupped varieties as narcissus.

The Royal Horticultural Society of Great Britain has separated daffodils (*Narcissus*) into 11 divisions, followed by commercial growers and exhibitors:

TRUMPET DAFFODILS: trumpet as long or longer than the perianth segments; available in yellow, white, and bicolors; one flower per stem. The outstanding example is 'King Alfred.'

LARGE-CUPPED DAFFODILS: trumpet more than one-third but less than equal to the length of the perianth segments; come in white or yellow and white with yellow, pink, or orange-red cup; one flower per stem.

SMALL-CUPPED DAFFODILS: cup not more than one-third the length of the perianth segments, available in white or white and yellow with colored cup; one flower per stem.

DOUBLE DAFFODILS: including all types with more than one layer of petals, regardless of the number of flowers per stem. Come in yellow or white or combination.

TRIANDRUS HYBRIDS: slender foliage and one to six flowers per stem. Subdivided according to whether cup is more or less than two-thirds the length of petals. Available in yellow, white, or white petals and yellow cup.

CYCLAMINEUS HYBRIDS: each stem bears one flower with petals curved back. Subdivided according to whether cup is more or less than two-thirds the length of petals. Available in yellow or cream petals and yellow cup.

JONQUILLA HYBRIDS: slender leaves and stems bearing two to six flowers each. Subdivided according to whether cup is more or less than two-thirds the length of petals. Available in yellow, ivory petals with pink cup, and yellow petals with red cup. Fragrant.

TAZETTA AND TAZETTA HYBRIDS: each stem bears a cluster of four to eight fragrant white flowers, usually with colored cups. Some are known as 'Chinese Sacred Lilies'.

POETICUS (OR POET'S NARCISSUS): usually bear one flower per stem, a fragrant white blossom with a shallow cup of a contrasting color.

SPECIES AND VARIETIES AND HYBRIDS: these are the small or miniature daffodils: *N. bulbocodium,* bright yellow; *N.b. citrinus,* lemon yellow; *N.b.* 'Conspicuus,' deep yellow, large trumpet; *N. tazetta* (usually sold as *N. canaliculatus*), the Polyanthus narcissus, with small white perianth segments, and golden cups; *N. cyclamineus,* lemon yellow perianth segments, bright yellow tubular trumpet; *N. jonquilla,* the sweetly fragrant yellow jonquil, with flowers in clusters; *N. asturiensis* (sold as *N.* 'Minimus'), the smallest trumpet daffodil; *N. triandrus*, the exquisite angel's tears, with clusters of small white flowers with reflexed perianths.

MISCELLANEOUS: all daffodils not falling into any of the foregoing divisions, including varieties with split cups and hybrids of the petticoat daffodil.

Use: One of the joys of growing daffodils is the number of ways in which you can use them in the garden and in containers:

• Small-cupped daffodils are effective under birches or flowering fruit trees — such as early flowering plum, cherry, or crabapple. Yellow trumpet daffodils look striking in front of citrus trees (a combination only for mild winter climates, of course).

• Shrubs like snow white bridal wreath *(Spiraea prunifolia* 'Plena') or *S. thunbergii* and daffodils go beautifully together in gardens or in arrangements. Early daffodils and forsythia make a cheery combination. The small-cupped daffodils and Persian lilac or *Viburnum burkwoodii* are excellent companions.

• Daffodils are highly successful planted among and under ground covers such as ajuga, euonymus, ivy, thyme, and vinca. They add color and vertical interest while the ground covers are becoming established; after a year or two, it may be necessary to thin the ground cover plants in the immediate vicinity of the bulbs.

• Jonquils thrive in cool, moist places, so plant them on the banks of pools and streams where their blooms can be reflected.

• Miniature species and hybrid daffodils are ideal for rock gardens and close-up situations, as in patio insets, raised beds, at the base of container grown trees or shrubs, or in containers of their own.

Culture: The accepted planting time for daffodils is from late August (or as early in the fall as bulbs can be obtained) to November (where weather permits). Tests show that planting bulbs as soon as possible after digging and curing insures stronger root systems and top growth the first year. And as a result of food from leaves being returned to the bulb at the end of the season, a vigorous, productive bulb is assured.

When buying daffodil bulbs, look for heavy, solid bulbs with basal plates unmarred by mechanical injuries or insects. For the best bulbs, buy number one double nose bulbs; the next best is the number two double nose. The latter size will give two or more flowers of good size to each bulb.

Plant large daffodil bulbs 5 to 6 inches deep (measure from the shoulder, or rounded portion of the bulb, not from the tip of the slender portion called the neck); if you set them 8 inches apart, you won't have to divide them for at least two or three years. Plant the next size smaller bulbs 4 to 5 inches deep and 6 inches apart, smaller ones 3 to 4 inches deep and the same distance apart. The general recommendation is to plant slightly deeper in sandy soils,

and shallower in heavy clay soils. Some growers gauge planting depths according to the following scale based on the depth of the bulb from the base to the top: three times the depth of the bulb for average or medium-heavy soils; deeper for light soils, shallower for heavy soils.

Although daffodils prefer a deep, fertile, well-drained sandy loam, they will perform well in heavier soils with good drainage. If your soil tends to hold too much water, lighten it with humus. Place a cushion of sand directly under each bulb when you plant it. If your soil is poor, thoroughly incorporate complete fertilizers into the planting area before setting out bulbs.

Planting under high branching, deciduous trees is usually successful since practically full sun is available during the time the flowers are developing and shade provided later in the season by leafed-out branches will keep flowers from burning.

In warmer climates where the ground is apt to be dry, thoroughly water daffodils immediately after planting to settle the soil and get the bulbs off to a good start. If fall rains arrive on schedule, it probably will not be necessary to water again before the blooming season. But in such sections of the country as the Southwest, where autumns are warm and winters are dry, plantings will need additional soakings. You can hardly give daffodils too much water when they are in full growth. In coldest areas, mulch daffodil plantings.

After daffodils bloom, let the foliage ripen naturally. The best time to lift and divide crowded plantings is immediately after the leaves are ripened. If you must move daffodils during the growing season, lift entire clumps with a spading fork and try to keep the soil intact around the roots. Replant clumps immediately and water in thoroughly.

If properly planted in deep, loose, fertile soil, daffodil bulbs can be left undisturbed for a number of years and still bloom freely each season. When the flowers get smaller and fewer in number, it's time to divide the bulbs.

When separating bulbs after digging, don't break away forcibly any bulblets that are still tightly joined to the mother bulb. The basal plates of the bulblet will not separate from that of the mother bulb; a bulblet without a basal plate will not grow, but will decay in the ground. Bulblets which break away easily should be removed and planted; any that are small and from unhealthy bulbs should be discarded.

Daffodils' most serious pest is the narcissus bulb fly. When infested with the whitish or yellowish-white larvae of the bulb fly, bulbs become soft, have brown scars on their outer scales, and fail to grow. The adult fly looks like a small bumblebee. The female lays eggs on leaves and necks of bulbs; the young grubs enter the scales and bore into the bulbs, opening the way for rots by fungi and bacteria.

Nerine

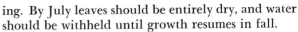

Bulb. Semi-hardy or tender.

Nerines are fall blooming South African bulbs that belong to the amaryllis family. Their uniquely beautiful, funnel-shaped flowers with six spreading segments reflexed at the tips are borne in rounded clusters on 12 to 18-inch stalks. Blooms are mostly in shades of pink or red, although there are hybrids in other colors. Strap-shaped leaves usually appear with or after the flowers; some are evergreen, others deciduous.

N. bowdenii. This is the hardiest species, with glossy green leaves 1 inch or less wide and 6 to 12 inches long. Flowers are soft pink with a darker pink line down the center of each segment and number 8 to 12 in a loose cluster at the top of a stout 2-foot stem. Leaves come out a month or two before the flowers and remain after bloom until the following spring or early summer, when they yellow and die down. Forms of *N. bowdenii,* some taller and with larger flower clusters, come in deeper pink with gold and silver sheen, pale crimson, and cherry red. This species alone is hardy enough to grow in western Oregon and Washington.

N. curvifolia 'Fothergillii Major.' Magnificent clusters of scarlet flowers overlaid with a shimmering gold, further enhanced with long exserted filaments topped by greenish yellow anthers, make this a most exciting plant. Bloom stalks are 18 inches high; the blue-green leaves grow to 12 inches long.

N. sarniensis. Guernsey lily. This remarkably handsome nerine has large clusters of iridescent crimson flowers on 2-foot stalks. Broad, strap-shaped leaves appear immediately after the flowers.

Use: Although nerines can be grown outdoors in mild climate gardens, they are generally grown in pots indoors or in a cool greenhouse in cold areas.

Culture: Plant the bulbs in sandy loam with peat moss or leaf mold, and bonemeal added. Some dealers offer bulbs of nerine throughout the year, but August to October (just as the bulbs are beginning to grow) are particularly good months to plant them.

Nerines flower best when they are potbound. Place one bulb in a 4-inch pot, three in a 5 or 6-inch pot. Set the bulb so that only the lower half is covered with soil.

Wait until you see signs of the flower stalk before watering, then water regularly through winter and spring. During the spring, as the weather warms, feed at monthly intervals with complete liquid fertilizer. In May, move pots outdoors into a lightly shaded spot and lengthen intervals between watering. By July leaves should be entirely dry, and water should be withheld until growth resumes in fall.

Do not repot nerine bulbs until they become crowded—this usually takes at least three or four years. An annual top-dressing of potting mix applied just before growth begins in the fall, as well as occasional feeding as mentioned above, is sufficient to keep the plant healthy.

In mild climates, plant nerines in sunny borders in perfectly drained soil, setting the bulbs 3 inches deep. The longer they are established, the better they bloom. It should not be necessary to lift and divide bulbs for several years.

Ornithogalum

Bulb. Hardy, semi-hardy, or tender.

Singled out for mention here are just a handful of the more than 100 species of ornithogalums that grow wild in Africa, Asia, and Europe. The selection includes the most readily available (*O. arabicum* and *O. umbellatum*) and three other species usually carried only by specialists dealing in unusual bulbs.

Ornithogalums' white, yellow, and (less rarely) red flowers are star-shaped, often fragrant, and held in handsome clusters. Most of them bloom in April and May. The leaves, which vary in different species from strap-shaped and fairly broad to narrow or linear, frequently tend to be floppy and untidy looking. Several species are unusually invasive.

O. arabicum. This is one of the finest and most popular ornithogalums. Its large handsome clusters of 2-inch, white, waxy-textured flowers are centered with lustrous, beady, black pistils that prompted early plantsmen to call this species the "Arab's eye." Two-foot bloom stalks stand above the leaves which are also 2 feet long but tend to flop languidly. Bulbs are 1½ inches in diameter. This bulb blooms freely in western Oregon and Washington, but will not flower the second year: bulbs require a hot soil to form the embryo flower.

O. arabicum is grown outdoors in all but coldest areas, where it is treated as an indoor or window plant. But its main forte is as a beautiful cut flower.

O. balansae, an attractive dwarf species from Asia Minor, has basal leaves and small clusters of white, green-striped flowers on very short stems. It blooms in early March or April, depending on climate, and is an excellent rock garden or border plant.

O. caudatum. (Pregnant onion, sea onion.) A curious plant, producing a green bulb over 4 inches in diameter. The strap-shaped, floppy leaves are 18 to 24 inches long. A stout, 2 to 4-foot stalk is topped in May with a cluster of 50 to 100 small, white, green-centered flowers. The pregnant onion is an interesting pot plant because of the way it produces new bulbs beneath the skin of the old.

O. thyrsoides. Chincherinchee. Tapering, compact clusters of white, star-like, 2-inch flowers with brownish green centers top 2-foot stems. As the blooms fade, they become grayish in color. Bright green upstanding leaves are 2 inches wide and 10 to 12 inches long. This species has large, globe-shaped bulbs. Although considered fairly tender, *O. thyrsoides* has been grown successfully through cold winters when planted in sheltered south or southwest locations and mulched during the winter. Familiar flower of South Africa's southwestern Cape, chincherinchee long ago won fame as a cut flower capable of surviving shipment when still in bud—and without water—from its native country to European florists.

O. umbellatum. Star-of-Bethlehem. Here is the best known ornithogalum, once widely planted and still a familiar sight in older gardens where it has run wild along with weeds. One-foot stems bear clusters of 1-inch-wide, white flowers striped green on the outside; narrow leaves are 1 foot long; the bulbs measure 1½ inches in diameter. Ingratiating, hardy, easily grown in sun or part shade, star-of-Bethlehem has outlived its welcome in many gardens by increasing too rapidly and ranging too far. The flowers last well when cut but close at night.

Use: Best uses are given for each species.

Culture: Plant bulbs in good, porous soil in sun or half shade in September or early October. Set smaller bulbs (1½ inches in diameter) 2 to 3 inches deep; larger (4-inch) bulbs 4 to 6 inches deep except for *O. caudatum* which should be planted with the top two-thirds above the soil surface. Lift and divide the bulbs when plantings become crowded.

Oxalis

Bulb or Rhizome.
Tender or semi-hardy.

For good reason, many warm-climate gardeners are wary of any member of this fantastically prolific genus (it contains over 800 species). When planted in the garden, some, such as the well-known Bermuda buttercup *(O. pes-caprae)* and *O. corniculata,* spread underground or by ejected seeds that cover a wide area. Of several

kinds offered by bulb specialists, the following are especially recommended:

O. adenophylla. Unlike many oxalis, this species forms a compact rosette of leaves (divided into 12 to 22 leaflets) that is attractive in itself. Lavender-pink flowers with deeper veins are 1½ inches across. Quite hardy.

O. bowiei. Showy pink or rose-purple flowers are 1½ to 2 inches across. Leaves are cloverlike.

O. hirta. Considered superior, this species has large, bright rose-pink blooms in winter. Cloverlike leaves are small and dainty.

Use: The more refined and easily controlled kinds of oxalis certainly have their place, especially for pots and hanging baskets. Gardeners in the East and Midwest appreciate them as winter-blooming house plants. Oxalis have five-petaled, white, yellow, pink, or rose-purple flowers that sometimes close at night and on overcast days.

Culture: Plant bulbs or rhizomes in August or September, setting them about 2 inches deep in full sun or light shade (outdoors only in mild-winter areas). Plant in pots in a spongy, well-drained soil mix and place in sun. Give the plant plenty of water when it is in active growth. After the bloom period, start withholding water and gradually let bulbs dry.

Polianthes Tuberosa

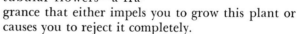

(Tuberose)
Tuber. Tender or semi-hardy.

The tuberose, a Mexican native, is famous principally for the exotic fragrance of its small, white, tubular flowers—a fragrance that either impels you to grow this plant or causes you to reject it completely.

The blooms, loosely arranged in spikelike clusters on 2 to 3-foot stems, appear from early summer to fall. Basal leaves are long, narrow and grasslike. Tuberoses come in single and double forms; although the singles are more graceful, the double form called 'The Pearl' is most widely available.

Use: Plant tuberoses in borders, raised beds, or containers: determine their location by whether you enjoy fragrance close by or wafted from a distance. In mild-winter areas, they make effective companions for such subtropicals as alocasia, caladium, colocasia, and coleus—all of which prosper under similar growing conditions. Tuberoses make excellent cut flowers if you enjoy their heady fragrance.

Culture: The long slender bulb-like tubers, about 1½ inches in diameter and 2 inches long, can be planted in the garden or in pots. A sound live tuber always shows signs of green at the growing tip. In colder climates, gardeners start them indoors in flats of moist peat or sphagnum moss in the same way they start tuberous begonias or cannas.

Wherever you live, there is no point in planting tuberoses outdoors until after the ground has warmed up, since they must have a steady, adequate supply of heat in order to grow and flower. Select a warm, sheltered spot in part shade; provide a well drained sandy loam to which you add ¼ part of peat moss, ground bark, well-rotted manure, or other organic matter.

Set tubers 2 inches deep and 4 to 6 inches apart. Water enough to moisten the planting bed. When leaves appear, start watering regularly and thoroughly, continuing throughout the active growing period. If soil or water in your area tends to be alkaline, counteract it by applying an acid-base fertilizer. Tubers bloom about four months after planting.

When the leaves begin turning yellow in autumn, withhold water, lift the tubers, and store them in a warm dry place over the winter. Tuberoses do not always bloom a second year. Cold-climate gardeners sometimes dig and pot up plants from the garden before frost and put them in a sunny window; they will bloom in November or December.

To grow in pots, plant three tubers in a 6-inch pot. Ideally, potted tubers require bottom heat (60° to 70°) to encourage strong root growth. If the soil mix is thoroughly moist when tubers are potted, it should not be necessary to water until the leaves appear. After top growth is up, provide lots of moisture and continue until the plant is through blooming. When foliage starts yellowing, follow the directions given above.

Ranunculus Asiaticus

(Persian buttercup, Turban buttercup) Tuber. Semi-hardy.

Ranunculus flowers look like large double buttercups (they are in the same genus); some strains have large blooms that remind you of smaller camellias. They come in yellows, oranges, reds, rose-pinks, dusty pinks, cream, and white; stems are 18 to 24 inches tall.

One of the finest and best known strains is Tecolote; a recent introduction is the El Rancho strain.

Use: Ranunculus add cheerful late spring color to borders in Western mild-climate gardens (they bloom later in western Oregon and Washington). They are particularly successful in large pots, tubs, or raised beds. Most of all, ranunculus are superb cut flowers.

Culture: Cultural requirements of *R. asiaticus* are similar to those of *Anemone coronaria*. In order to develop their flowers, they need cool nights and sunny, but not hot, days. They must have a fertile, well-drained soil containing considerable humus and lots of moisture while they are growing. Little wonder that the finest ranunculus are grown in Western desert climates during winter months when nights are cold and days are bright and abundant water is supplied by irrigation.

In cold climates, these conditions can be provided in greenhouses during winter and early spring. However, in these areas where planting outdoors must be delayed until after spring frosts, ranunculus rarely have a chance to develop good flowers before the weather becomes hot.

In mild-winter climates, plant the tubers in October and November (in western Oregon and Washington, plant them in November or mid-February). Select a well-drained site fully exposed to the sun and plant in a soil mixture made up of equal parts of good loam, coarse sand, and humus. Set tubers 2 inches under the surface with the prongs pointing downward.

The small, claw-like tubers are dry and bone hard when you buy them. They will not form roots until they have absorbed sufficient moisture to make them plump. Delay in rooting often causes tubers to rot. To avoid this delay, some gardeners in warm, dry sections soak the tubers 3 or 4 hours; others roll them in a wet towel for two or three days before planting. Or you can plant the untreated tubers in ground that has been carefully prepared and thoroughly moistened so that further watering will not be needed before the leaves appear above the surface. It is usually necessary to cover the young growing plants to protect them from birds.

Tubers will plump up naturally in the warm, moist earth; once growth is active, there is little danger of rot. In western Oregon and Washington, where the soil is wet at planting time, it is inadvisable to soak the tubers.

After the plants are through blooming and have become dry, lift them, cut off the tops, and store the tubers in a dry, cool place. Or, as many gardeners do, treat ranunculus as annuals and make new plantings each year. Western nurseries sell them as transplants in flats in the fall months. You can also start your own plants from seed in summer or set out the plants in fall at the same time as you would tubers.

Schizostylis Coccinea

(Crimson flag, Kaffir lily)
Rhizome. Tender or semi-hardy.

Comparatively little known, this South African plant is available only from specialists and has been planted mostly in mild climate sections of the West. Natively the plants grow wild over large areas—mostly in high altitude peaty swamps. The clumps of plants rest on tufts of vegetation, and the roots are only a few inches above water.

Spikes of showy crimson, starlike, 2½-inch flowers appear at the top of slender 18 to 24-inch stems, opening successively from the bottom to the top during the blooming season in October and November. The leaves, reminiscent of narrow gladiolus foliage, are evergreen and 18 inches tall. A horticultural variety of schizostylis, called 'Mrs. Hegarty,' with red or rose-pink blooms is superior to the species.

Use: This is an ideal cut flower: attractive, unusual, and long lasting (each flower lasts about four days; others follow).

Culture: Plant the rhizomatous roots in well prepared soil in sun or light shade (in hot climates). Since this plant grows natively in moist places and in soil rich in humus, add peat moss or leaf mold in the planting area and give the plants lots of water during the growing season. When the clumps become thick, divide them in spring, leaving at least five shoots on each division.

Scilla

(Squill, bluebell)
Bulb. Hardy and semi-hardy.

For many gardeners, scillas begin and end with the familiar, spring-blooming Spanish bluebell (S. hispanica) and the English bluebell or wood hyacinth (S. nonscripta). But there are other worthwhile scillas that flower in the spring and some summer and fall-blooming ones.

Scillas have bell-shaped or sometimes starlike flowers in blue, purple, pink, and white, borne in terminal clusters on leafless stalks. The basal leaves are strap-shaped.

S. bifolia. First among the small, brilliant blue flowering bulbs of spring is this charming south European mountain species that blooms as the snow melts. Up to eight turquoise starlike flowers (also white, pale purplish pink, and violet-blue varieties), about an inch across, are borne on 8-inch stems.

S. hispanica (formerly called S. campanulata). Spanish bluebell. This native of Spain and Portugal is the most widely grown species. It is a hardy, vigorous, prolific, and easy-to-grow bulb, its sturdy 20-inch stems bearing about a dozen crisp, ½-inch to ¾-inch, nodding bells. The blue form is justly most popular; there are also white, pink, and rose forms. In some areas, this scilla blooms quite late in spring.

S. nonscripta (formerly called S. nutans). English bluebell. Wood hyacinth. This appealing Western European native has become one of England's landmark flowers, carpeting woods in May with its misty blue. Again, there are white and pink forms, but it's the blue one that make this scilla famous. The graceful, nodding, sweet scented bells, smaller and narrower than those of S. hispanica, top 1-foot-high stalks—much like loose-spiked hyacinth stalks.

S. peruviana. Peruvian scilla (the common name is misleading, since the plant is native of the Mediterranean area). To look at it, you'd hardly suspect this plant to be a scilla. Its bluish purple, starlike flowers—50 or more in a large dome-shaped cluster—appear on leafless 10 or 12-inch stalks. The long, floppy, strap-shaped leaves die down after the flowers bloom in May and June. This is the least hardy scilla.

S. tubergeniana is another early-blooming species, keeping company with the first snowdrops and offering its pale blue bells as a complement to the golden yellow blooms of winter aconite. Four or more flowers appear on 4-inch stalks; each bulb sends up three or more stalks.

S. sibirica. Siberian squill. If this delightful little scilla grew as thriftily in warm winter areas as it does in cold, it would undoubtedly be the most popular of all scillas. In early spring, it displays dainty, flaring bells of intense blue on 3 to 6-inch stems.

Use: Spanish bluebells grow freely and increase rapidly under deciduous trees or under high branching evergreen trees that don't cast too dense shade.

Siberian scillas make delightful blue drifts under deciduous azaleas, forsythia, and flowering quince. For a clean sparkling blue and white combination, plant interlocking groups of these small scillas with snowdrops or wood anemones.

Scilla peruviana makes handsome substantial clumps in rock gardens or mixed borders, although some gardeners prefer not to use them in prominent positions because of the untidy appearance of the foliage as it turns yellow shortly after bloom. It is an attractive pot plant; in colder areas, it is sometimes forced in greenhouses.

Culture: Plant scillas in September or October in sun or in part shade in good garden soil. Set bulbs of *S. hispanica* 3 inches deep; *S. sibirica* 2 to 3 inches deep; *S. peruviana* 4 to 6 inches deep. All require lots of moisture during the growing season.

Although scillas grow and increase rapidly, it is best to leave them undisturbed for several years before lifting and dividing. *S. hispanica* and *S. sibirica* self-sow and can also be propagated from offsets. Bulbs of *S. peruviana* remain dormant for a very short time after the leaves wither; if replanting is necessary, do it before the bulbs show new growth.

To grow in pots, plant six bulbs of *S. sibirica* in a 5-inch pot; use a 6-inch pot for six bulbs of *S. hispanica*. Peruvian scilla bulbs are larger; place one in a 6-inch pot or three bulbs in a 9 or 10-inch pot.

Sinningia Speciosa

(Gloxinia)
Tuber. Tender.

The luxurious tropical splendor of gloxinias (formerly called *Gloxinia speciosa*) has lured many gardeners into thinking of this indoor plant as capricious and temperamental. Yet many gardeners find them no more difficult to manage than tuberous begonias.

Gloxinia plants are crowned with large, bell-shaped flowers, sometimes double, ruffled along the edges and glowing in gorgeous blues, purples, pinks, reds, and pure white. Some blooms are curiously dotted with dark spots; others have blotches of solid colors. The green, fuzzy large leaves look and feel like soft velvet.

Use: Gloxinias, unlike begonias, are not usually treated as garden plants. To keep them happy outside of their native Brazilian jungles, you must grow them in greenhouses or as house plants. They want lots of light but require shade from strong sunshine. Night temperatures can go down to 50°, but 63° to 65° is considered ideal. Gloxinias enjoy humidity, resent drafts and dry atmosphere. But when they're in bloom you can give them lots of air and move them onto covered terraces, patios, and porches. These plants also perform satisfactorily under fluorescent lights in basements and apartments.

Culture: Tubers of gloxinias are available in some garden supply stores between December and March. The shipping season depends on how early growers can force them into dormancy.

Set tubers individually 1 inch deep in pots just large enough to accommodate them. Use the same mixture recommended for potting up seedlings, adding a teaspoon of complete fertilizer for each 5-inch pot. It's a good idea to mix up a large batch of potting soil ahead of time so that it is available and has had time to break down into a mellow compost.

After potting tubers, water sparingly until the first leaves appear. When roots have formed, increase watering. Apply water around the base of the plant or from below. Do not water on the leaves, for this causes them to rot. Be careful not to overwater.

When pots are filled with roots, shift the plants into larger pots. Flowers and foliage decrease in size when plants become potbound.

You grow gloxinias from seed in the same way as you grow tuberous begonias. Place a mixture of ¾ leaf mold and ¼ peat moss in a flat or seed pan (shallow pot) after lining the bottom with 2 inches of broken crock or gravel. After you have firmed and smoothed the surface to a perfect level, soak the container from below, then sow the seed. Do not cover the fine seed with soil. After sowing, cover the pot with a piece of glass and a sheet of paper. Germination usually starts in about 10 days. When seedlings appear, remove the paper but do not expose to sunlight. In four or five days, remove the glass also so that seedlings will not get spindly.

When seedlings are large enough to handle, prick them off into another seed pan or flat, spacing them about 3 inches apart. Use a light, porous, spongy potting mixture containing one part coarse, sharp sand and two parts peat moss or ground bark (or peat moss or ground bark mixed with well-decayed leaf mold).

As the plants grow larger, shift them into 4, 5, or 6-inch pots, depending on their size. They will begin flowering in eight or nine months after sowing. Because seedlings come into bloom at irregular intervals, you can expect to have flowers for many months.

If you want more plants of a certain variety of gloxinia, make leaf cuttings. Use partly matured medium-sized leaves with a small portion of the leaf stock attached. Insert into sand and keep it on the slightly dry side. Bottom heat is necessary for quick rooting.

You can also increase gloxinias by taking off little shoots from the side of a plant and potting them in the same soil mix as for seedlings. These offsets should have about four leaves. Because they are more advanced, offsets bloom earlier than plants from leaf cuttings.

For rapid growth and large flowers, fertilize gloxinias regularly. Start feeding seedlings after they are established in their first pots and continue throughout the growing and flowering periods. Some growers fertilize their plants every two weeks with 1 tablespoon fish emulsion to 1 quart of water.

Do not apply fertilizer when plants are dry. Water the plants first, then fertilize a few hours later.

After flowering, gradually withhold water until the plants are completely dormant. Store the tubers in a cool, dark place in which the temperature is held to about 50°. Keep tubers slightly moist—just enough to prevent shriveling. In January or February, when gloxinias show signs of starting into active growth, shake off the old soil and repot them.

Snowdrop, see *Galanthus.*

Snowflake, see *Leucojum.*

Sparaxis Tricolor

(Harlequin flower)
Corm. Tender to semi-hardy.

Sparaxis, a gay plant from the Cape of Good Hope, delights gardeners who like vital, sparkling colors. Small, funnel-shaped, gladiolus-like flowers, in spikelike clusters on 12-inch stems, come in yellows, blues, purples, reds, and white, usually blotched and splashed with contrasting colors.

Sparaxis blooms for a long period in late spring. Early flowers last well and new ones come along to stretch the flowering season from six to eight weeks.

Use: Mass them in a narrow bed between a walk and wall, in crevices in a rock garden, in the cutting garden; or plant in containers.

If planted close together in groups, the slender plants hold each other up and the flowers make solid masses of color.

Culture: Plant corms in fall in mild winter climates, setting them 2 inches deep and 2 or 3 inches apart. If you want to take a chance on planting sparaxis outdoors in fall (October to early November) in cold-winter areas, select the most protected spot in the garden. Plant in a light sandy soil that is perfectly drained. Set the corms 4 inches deep, mulch with peat moss or leaf mold, and superimpose a layer of straw or evergreen boughs—to be removed in spring when the plants start to grow through the blanket of humus underneath.

Of course, a safer method in cold winter areas is to plant the corms in pots in fall and keep the pots in a protected place through the severe weather (as in a greenhouse or coldframe insulated with fiberglass). Provide light and warmth when plants start to grow and display them when they bloom.

Sprekelia Formosissima

(Jacobean lily,
St. James lily, Aztec lily)
Bulb. Semi-hardy.

Brilliant crimson, 4-inch flowers, held singly on stout 12-inch stems, distinguish this Mexican, early-summer blooming plant (formerly called *Amaryllis formosissima*). The curiously shaped blooms have three erect segments and three lower ones which are rolled together at the base to form a tube, then separate again into three drooping segments. Stamens protruding from the tube are tipped with large pendulous anthers. Strap-shaped leaves are about a foot long.

Use: For dramatic color in borders or rock gardens, plant five or more bulbs in a group. Sprekelia is also a superb pot plant.

Culture: Outdoors, set bulbs 3 or 4 inches deep and 8 inches apart in light, enriched, well drained soil in full sun. Plant in fall where winters are mild. In severe-winter areas, set out bulbs in late spring, lift plants in fall when foliage yellows, and store for the winter (with dry tops left on) in a frost-free location.

To grow in pots, plant one bulb in a 4-inch pot. Culture is similar to that for amaryllis except that temperatures should be maintained at 5° to 10° lower. Sprekelia will bloom beautifully indoors in rooms that are kept only moderately warm. Repot bulbs every three or four years.

Sternbergia Lutea

Bulb. Hardy.

Although it is sometimes called the autumn daffodil, this bulb from the Mediterranean region by no means looks like a daffodil. Rather, it resembles an oversized golden yellow crocus about 1¾ inches long. Blooms stand singly and erect on 6 to 9-inch stems. The narrow 6 to 12-inch-long leaves appear in fall at the same time as the flowers and remain green for several months after blooms are gone.

Use: Sternbergia's cheerful yellow enhances borders, rock gardens and walls, and niches beside pools. The crocuslike blooms also add an element of surprise among low growing succulents or other ground-hugging plants. Sternbergias are delightful cut flowers and can be grown in containers.

Culture: Plant bulbs as soon as available, in August or September. Set bulbs 4 inches deep and 6 to 8 inches apart in light, well drained soil in a sunny location. In colder climates, where sternbergia is not very permanent or reliable in its bloom, grow it in the most protected position possible. After bulbs become crowded lift, divide, and replant in August.

Tigridia Pavonia

(Tiger flower, Mexican shell flower) Bulb. Tender.

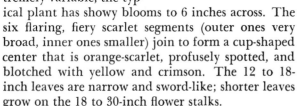

Flamboyant summer-flowering tigridias are natives from Mexico to Chile. Although extremely variable, the typical plant has showy blooms to 6 inches across. The six flaring, fiery scarlet segments (outer ones very broad, inner ones smaller) join to form a cup-shaped center that is orange-scarlet, profusely spotted, and blotched with yellow and crimson. The 12 to 18-inch leaves are narrow and sword-like; shorter leaves grow on the 18 to 30-inch flower stalks.

Although individual blooms last but a single day, others follow in regular succession over a period of many weeks from July into August. Hybrids of *T. pavonia* are available in shades of red, salmon, pink, yellow, and white, usually with darker markings.

Use: For bold, gay splashes in borders or rock gardens, plant in groups of 10 or more bulbs. Interplant with tulips or with clumps of spring-blooming iris for follow-up color in summer. Surround colonies of tigridia with a ground cover of blue lobelia if you enjoy warm-cool combinations.

Culture: Wait to plant until after the weather has warmed up in spring. Set bulbs 2 to 4 inches deep and 4 to 8 inches apart in rich, porous soil in a sunny location. In hot summer climates, select a location with afternoon shade.

To grow in containers, plant six bulbs in an 8 or 9-inch pot—or box of equivalent size. Keep the newly potted corms at a temperature of 50° and water only lightly. After bulbs have formed strong roots and leaves poke through the soil, increase the temperature to 55° and water more generously.

Well established tigridias growing in the ground may require a thorough watering once a week. Diluted solutions of a complete fertilizer applied weekly or every 10 days are beneficial for tigridias after they are in active growth.

In mild climates where the ground does not freeze, tigridias may be left in the ground through the winter. In colder sections of the country, dig the bulbs after the leaves turn yellow, dry off all surplus moisture, and store in dry sand, soil, sawdust, or vermiculite in a cool, frost-free place. In digging, be very careful not to break the bulbs apart; do not divide until just before planting in the spring. Tigridias should be divided every three or four years.

Tigridias are quite easy to grow from seed. If you sow seed early, you may get bloom that summer.

In warm dry areas, red spider mites often attack tigridias, causing yellow or whitish streaks on the leaves. Spray regularly, starting when the leaves are a few inches tall, with a miticide or with malathion.

Triteleia uniflora, see *Ipheion uniflorum.*

Tritonia

(Montbretia) Corm. Semi-hardy.

A showy South African plant, sometimes called montbretia, tritonia is related to freesia, gladiolus, ixia, and sparaxis and has similar uses and cultural requirements.

T. crocata is often called flame freesia because its 2-inch, orange-red, funnel-shaped flowers resemble freesias. Branched flower stems grow to 12 inches above a basal tuft of narrow, grasslike leaves. The variety 'Princess Beatrix,' has deep orange flowers.

T. hyalina differs from *T. crocata* in that its bright orange flower segments are narrower and have a transparent area near the base. It is also lower growing.

Use: Tritonias thrive in sunny pockets in rock gardens, make bright splashes of color in the foreground of shrubbery and perennial borders and among succulents, are splendid cut flowers, and can be grown in pots.

Culture: Plant tritonias in fall in light, rich well-drained soil in full sun. Set corms 3 to 4 inches deep and 6 inches apart. In cold areas, heavy mulching will often carry them over the winter. Or you can lift corms in the fall and store in the same way as gladiolus. In mild sections, leave corms in the ground and lift and divide them when they become crowded. After flowering, let tritonias dry off somewhat.

Tuberose, see *Polianthes tuberosa.*

Tuberous Begonia, see *Begonia*

Tulbaghia Violacea

(Society garlic)
Cormous. Semi-hardy.

This South African plant has a most appropriate common name. The society label is justified by the attractive clusters of small, star-like, rosy lilac flowers on 18-inch stems that keep blooming for months—from late spring to fall in warmer sections. And the narrow gray-green leaves that grow in tight clumps and give off a strong odor of onions when crushed produce the association with garlic. The variety 'Silver Lace' has variegated foliage.

Use: In mild climates, tulbaghia is a long-suffering, practically indestructible border or edging plant, is attractive in rock gardens, and is a handsome pot plant (the best way to grow in a cold winter climate.)

Culture: Tulbaghia isn't fussy; simply give it ordinary garden soil and full sun. If you want to try growing it in the open ground in colder areas, plant it in light, well drained soil in the most sheltered position possible and mulch in the winter with straw or leaves. Divide clumps when they become large and crowded.

Tulipa

(Tulip)
Bulb. Hardy.

Among bulbous plants, the tulip is one of the finest prizes ever to come out of that rich botanical hunting ground extending from the northern Mediterranean region through the Caucasus, north and central Asia, and east to China and Japan.

Most of the tulips we grow today have been classified into 23 divisions by the Royal General Dutch Bulb Growers Society in collaboration with the Royal Horticultural Society of England. This is not a botanical classification but primarily an aid to nurserymen, growers, show exhibitors, and catalog writers. It is also, of course, a convenience to gardeners. Here are the most important of these divisions:

SINGLE EARLY TULIPS. Tulips in this class have large single flowers in red, yellow, and white, on 10 to 16-inch stems. Although favorites for growing or forcing early indoors in pots, they can also be grown outside, where they bloom from March to mid-April, depending on climate and variety. They are not adapted to warm winter climates.

DOUBLE EARLY TULIPS. Double peony-like flowers—often measuring 4 inches across—grow on 6 to 12-inch stems. They come in much the same color range as the single early kinds and are forced for early bloom in containers. In colder climates they are also effective planted in masses in borders for spring bloom outside; except for a few species, they are usually the first to bloom. Because of their short stems, the flowers often get splashed with mud unless plants are mulched or grown under cover.

MENDEL TULIPS. The result of crosses between Darwin and 'Duc Van Tol' (a very early flowering class of tulips now superseded by the single and double early classes). They have single flowers on stems up to 20 inches tall and bloom later than the single and double early tulips but earlier than the Darwins. Varieties include red, pink, orange, yellow, and white.

TRIUMPH TULIPS. A class derived from crosses between single early tulips and the late May flowering kinds. They bloom earlier than the Darwins and have shorter, heavier stems, usually not over 20 inches. Available in red, white, yellow, and bicolors.

DARWIN TULIPS. These popular late flowering tulips form graceful, stately plants with large oval or egg-shaped blooms, square at the base, usually with rounded flower segments on straight stems up to 30 inches tall. Clear, beautiful colors come in a remarkably extensive range: white, yellow, orange, pink, red, mauve, lilac, purple, and maroon.

DARWIN HYBRIDS. This superb race of comparatively recent origin shows the influence of one parent, *T. fosteriana,* in its huge shining, brilliant flowers and that of the Darwins in its proud stance on strong 2-foot stems. And the bloom period conveniently occurs between the two. Varieties come in scarlet, red, and orange.

BREEDER TULIPS. Large, oval or globular flowers on sturdy stems up to 40 inches tall. Unusual colors, with orange, bronze, and purple predominating.

LILY-FLOWERED TULIPS. Graceful lily-shaped blooms, longer and narrower than those of the Darwins, with long, pointed flower segments, set this class apart. Formerly included in the Cottage tulip division, lily-flowered tulips have been set fairly recently into a separate division. These are among the most useful tulips for cutting and gardens, where they combine beautifully with other plants. The bloom period is about the same as that of the Darwin hybrids. You can choose from yellow, pink, red, and white varieties.

COTTAGE TULIPS. These exquisite tulips are descendants of older varieties found growing in old gardens in the British Isles and in Belgium and France. They are about the same size and height as the Darwins, with varying forms: long oval or egg-shaped, often with pointed flower segments. Colors include red, purple, yellow, pink, orange, and white.

REMBRANDT TULIPS. These are "broken" Darwin tulips—so-called because the flowers are streaked or variegated throughout with different colors.

BIZARRE TULIPS. This class is comprised of "broken" Breeder or Cottage tulips. Flowers have a yellow background striped or marked with bronze, brown, maroon, or purple.

BYBLOEMS (OR BIJBLOEMENS). These are "broken" Breeder or Cottage tulips that have a white background with markings of rose, lilac, or purple.

PARROT TULIPS. This class of May flowering tulips includes sports of solid colored varieties of regular form, with large, long, deeply fringed and ruffled blooms, striped, feathered, and flamed in various colors. Parrot tulips used to have weak, floppy stems, but today's varieties stand up well. Several varieties have the name Parrot, preceded by the name of the color of that particular variety: for instance, 'Black Parrot,' 'Blue Parrot,' 'Ivory Parrot.'

DOUBLE LATE TULIPS. As the name implies, this class of tulips has double flowers that bloom late in the season. Often they are referred to as peony-flowered. Their extremely large, heavy blooms come in orange, yellow, rose, or white.

SPECIES AND SPECIES HYBRIDS. In the classification of tulips, three divisions are varieties and hybrids of *T. fosteriana, T. greigii,* and *T. kaufmanniana.*

T. fosteriana. This early flowering statuesque tulip has 4-inch blossoms on 8 to 20-inch stems. Hybridizers have never been able to develop a blossom as large as this wild species.

T. greigii. This outstanding species tulip is noted for its glorious array of blossoms, as well as for its beautifully mottled and marked leaves.

T. kaufmanniana. Called the waterlily tulip, this is one of the loveliest, earliest, and sturdiest of the species tulips, widely used in hybridizing. Medium-large blooms are creamy yellow, marked with red on the outside, revealing a bright yellow center when the flower segments open flat in the sun.

SPECIES AND BOTANICAL TULIPS. Varied in form and coloring, often small in stature (some are miniatures), usually early blooming, species tulips appeal especially to the adventurous gardener. You have to see these unusual tulips in flower to appreciate their rare and whimsical charm.

T. batalinii. Single, soft yellow flowers on 6 to 10-inch stem with linear leaves.

T. stellata chrysantha (also called *T. chrysantha*). An exquisite little Himalayan tulip—star-shaped when open; outside flower segments are pure rose-carmine merging to buff at the base; inside segments are pure buttercup yellow.

T. clusiana. This is the graceful lady or candy tulip, with slender, medium-sized blooms colored rosy red on the outside, creamy white inside. This is a good permanent tulip for areas with little winter chill.

T. eichleri. A striking, sculptured looking tulip with shining scarlet flowers and a jet-black center outlined with yellow.

T. linifolia. Glossy scarlet flowers have dark purple basal blotch. This is a charming companion for the yellow *T. batalinii,* which blooms at the same time.

T. marjolettii. Small, creamy white flowers are flaked and feathered soft pink on a slender stem.

T. praestans. Pure orange-scarlet flowers, often two to four to a stem, contrast beautifully with pale green leaves edged with dark red. This species produces magnificent splashes of color and is a very satisfactory garden plant.

T. tarda (usually called *T. dasystemon*). This is a most appealing little tulip with a cluster of as many as four flowers on each trailing, leafy stem. Segments of the star-shaped flowers are alternately greenish purple and white, with a green midrib and yellow base; the inside of the bloom is yellow on the lower half, white on the upper half.

Use: Well grown, well placed tulips, carefully selected according to color and kind, can make a tremendous impact on the spring garden. In mixed flower borders, use the Darwins with their proud form and clear colors, the Lily-flowering tulips with their delicate grace and pastel shades, and the Cottage tulips with their simple charm. All are most effective planted in groups or drifts—never in rows—of one color. Low, spring-flowering perennials (such as alyssum, arabis, aubrieta, iberis, and *Phlox divaricata*) make wonderful edgings or ground covers for these tulips.

A simpler scheme is to let tulips grow out of a solid mass of one kind of lower growing annuals, such as forget-me-not (*Myosotis*), baby-blue-eyes (*Nemophila*), sweet alyssum, or violas.